The Long Way Home

Stuart MacDonald

www.beyondsailing.co.uk

© 2014   Stuart MacDonald.

Stuart MacDonald has asserted his rights in accordance
with the Copyright, Designs and Patents Act 1988 to be
identified as the author of this work.

Published by   Stuart MacDonald

ISBN: 9781849146050

*For my family and the friends I
made along the way*

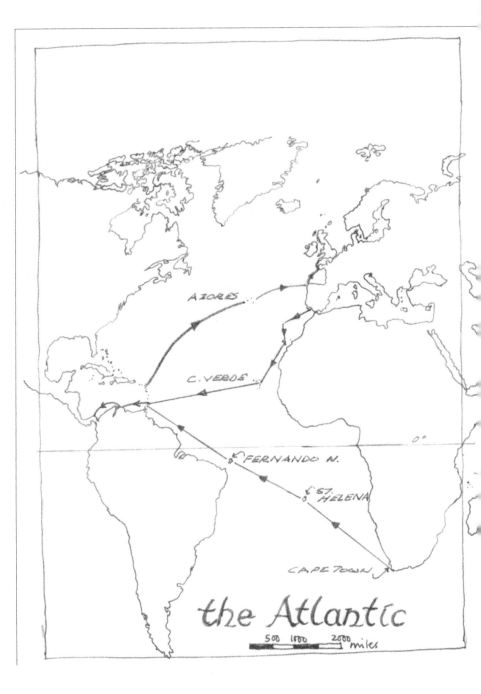

AZORES

C. VERDS

FERNANDO N.

ST. HELENA

CAPE TOWN

the Atlantic

500 1000 2000 miles

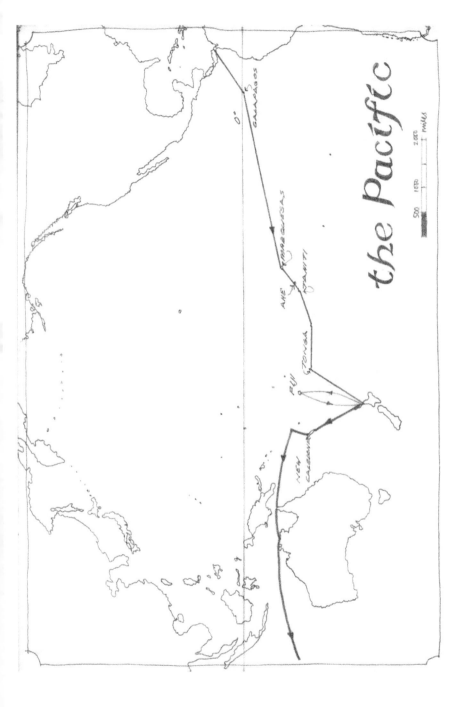

the Pacific

GALAPAGOS

0°

MARQUESAS
AHE
TAHITI

TONGA

FIJI

NEW CALEDONIA

500   1000   2000
miles

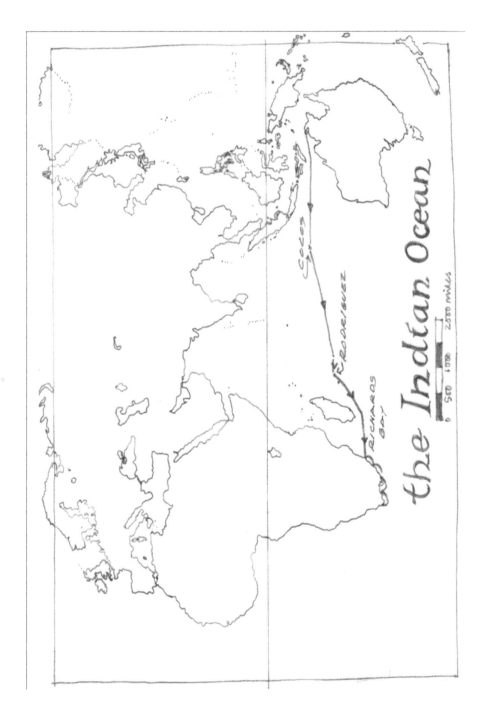
the Indian Ocean

BEYOND

Built in 1991

Length	11.6 metres
Beam	4.0 metres
Draft	2.0 metres

Foreword

DURING the course of the four year voyage described in The Long Way Home, I left the boat on three occasions. The first was to attend the wedding of my son, the second to attend the wedding of my nephew and the third to visit Argentina.

On each of these occasions I felt trapped in an unreal bubble; an artificial excision from the reality of life on board. I was browned, thin, weather-beaten and dressed in shore-going clothes which no longer fitted me; wearing shoes and socks instead of going barefoot - a modern Ancient Mariner, I was locked in my sea-going existence.

Like the Ancient Mariner, I needed to tell my story.

The Story

Letting Go

In the Beginning

SEOUL, South Korea, January 2009. It was way below freezing and a biting wind blew the snow into my face when I walked across Guanguam Square from the apartment towards my office. My left arm began to ache. I was working myself into the ground, running a very tough project and making good money but I was mentally exhausted. I had had enough.

Eighteen months of hard work, and a certain amount of planning later, I stepped off a bus in Brest into the wind and the drizzle and set off down the marina breakwater towards my boat, *Beyond*. I had a backpack, a holdall filled with books, a long plastic bag containing my new boom tent and a few bits of wood from the shed at home, which I thought might be useful. My arms were aching and I had to leave the plastic bag on the pontoon but I was within sight of the boat which was lying peacefully where I had left her.

It was wet and grey outside but dry and tidy down below. I dumped what I had and went back for the bag. With everything on board I sat down and drew breath. The boat was about as ready as I could make her. All the domestic arrangements were in place at home and there was nothing, apart from the present poor weather, to stop me going wherever I wanted for as long as I cared to wander. I put the kettle on. As a first step into the future

1

it was hardly momentous but all journeys have to start somewhere.

Many years before as a young seaman I had dreamt of doing an Atlantic circuit and, at one stage, I had owned a small cruising boat capable of it complete with the then obligatory paraffin stove, oil lamps and twin headsails. But I got shanghaied on a Glasgow tramp and by the time I got back to Scotland, after 14 months of hauling coal and phosphate round the Pacific, I had missed the window. Somehow after that life took over. The boat went and the long cruise plans went with it. Now, forty years on, I had a modest pension, chronic high blood pressure and two wonderful children now grown up. There was nothing to keep me at home. I was finally ready to go. I hung suspended between the world of work, which I was leaving, and the world of wandering which I was joining. I had spent nearly fifty years doing what I thought I ought to do and now I could pretty much do what I wanted. It was an odd feeling, like an animal in a zoo might feel after years of captivity when someone leaves the cage open and the chance to roam presents itself.

I had built up quite a collection of books about yacht cruising over the years of dreaming and I had brought some of them with me, the faded dates inside their covers spanning over 40 years. Like me they had moved afloat and would be setting off on the very kind of journey their authors had written about. The old classics by ground-breaking sailors like Harry Pidgeon, Hiscock, Slocum and Moitessier sat a dignified distance from the more up-to-date volumes, with their talk of satellite communication, essential medicines and the minimum amp hour capacity you need to run your freezer. Times had changed. *Beyond* is a good compromise between past and present and I had kept everything as simple as possible. She would probably be regarded as Spartan by today's American authors; with no freezer, water maker or air conditioning. How would I get by? I would soon find out.

I was all in favour of traditional seafaring skills and I had spent years navigating merchant ships with a sextant but I didn't have one anymore and, in a way, I regretted it. I had sold the instrument years ago when car, home and family had taken care of all my disposable income and I wanted some new sails for my dinghy. You do what seems right at the time and now I couldn't afford one. When you can buy a hand-held GPS and a clutch of AA batteries for a third of the price of a sextant, electronic back-up seemed the way to go and many ships have been lost because they couldn't get a sight. Life moves on. Naval surgeons used to saw the limbs off wounded seamen without any anaesthetic and dip the stumps in hot tar but that doesn't mean it's still the right way to do it.

Back home the shed had been painted, the little garden beaten into submission and the house closed up. Perhaps the most liberating feeling of all was that I had sold the car. I had squeezed enough medication out of the doctor to last a good few months and there was not really much else I could think of to do. I could go on preparing for ever and never get away but you can't make a twenty year old boat into a new one even if you had the cash, or a 64-year-old sailor into a teenager. I felt sure a few things would go wrong with both of us along the way. When people asked how long I was going for, I replied truthfully, that I didn't know but the real answer was that I would keep going until I had had enough, or couldn't handle the sailing anymore. I might get sick of the whole concept after a few months but I felt I had to find out.

I had a loose plan to follow - the usual route across Biscay and down the Spanish coast then over to Madeira, the Canaries and the West Indies. Beyond that, I had only a vague idea of where I would end up and I thought that if I found somewhere I really liked I would stay a while, seasonal weather permitting. The Pacific had always fascinated me but the problem of getting through the Panama Canal on my own worried me and I thought no more about it for a while. I would just let things take their course.

I had left the Clyde in early May and cruised down to Plymouth for the two-handed Round Britain and Ireland race, one of the great classics of short-handed racing. My co-skipper Angus and I got round in one piece but it was hard going. With a combined crew age of 126, we lacked the stamina of most entrants, and their grasp of technology, when all that seemed to matter was getting the internet weather files downloaded and into whatever performance management programme was loaded onto their boat's PC. At every stopover the talk had been of Grib files, optimum angles and polars and, in some way, it seemed to me that shorthanded distance racing had almost become a computer game. Angus and I had felt out of it, two old farts who still listened to the shipping forecast. I was glad to be doing no more racing.

A couple of weeks in the Yealm, Devon and in Falmouth followed. Falmouth is still the jumping off point for many would-be long distance cruisers and there were quite a few boats clearly intending to do the same as I was. The boats in the anchorage were a mixture of upmarket, generally immaculate heavy displacement cruisers, middle of the road boats like mine, and some distinctly rough-looking efforts. Further up towards Penryn lay a sorry collection of almost derelict craft, the department of broken dreams.

The owners seemed to span a similar range of apparent conditions and, I assumed, prosperity. I spotted one gent polishing his winches with a toothbrush, whilst his immaculately-clad wife sat in the cockpit reading a magazine and eating chocolates. I got some advice from one of the owners at the other end of the spectrum on where the best scrappy was to get a used alternator.

I left Falmouth one July evening and enjoyed an easy crossing to Brittany with the monitor doing all the work, and very little shipping to worry about. My brother Iain came along, but found that night channel crossings were not his forte; spending most of the trip in his bunk then emerging about breakfast time, spirits restored by the sight of the French coast.

Finally here I was, about to set off on a new life. There was nothing to hold me back. With the right forecast I had no excuse not to head off across the Bay of Biscay to Spain. I had no idea when or where it would all end, but I had put "Glasgow " on the stern so that I wouldn't forget where I started from and I hoped perhaps a few people would see that and stop and say hello.

It all lay ahead.

2

The Adventure Begins

The first step is the point of no return

On August 13 I let go the lines, slipped away from Camaret in northwestern France and sailed down through the Raz and round to Benodet where I stayed for a couple of days moored to a pontoon in the fast-flowing river waiting for a reasonable forecast to set off across the Bay of Biscay to Spain. There was some sort of music festival on and I wandered around very conscious of the fact that I was on my own in amongst a crowd of people clearly out to enjoy themselves. I was starting to worry that this might not be the most sociable of lifestyles. The marina was very expensive and I was keen to escape and get on with my new life which I felt should be a bit different from that of the other people on the cruising boats around me. I was, after all I thought, a full-time cruising man with plenty of time on my hands and free to roam to wherever I could get to. Somehow, sitting in a packed marina didn't quite fit and after two days with the wind in the northwest I set off heading for La Coruna.

The first day wasn't too bad. The boat kept moving, the monitor steered and I sat and felt generally good about things, though there were a few nervous moments. It was a while since I had made any serious passages alone but the next morning the wind dropped and, for a while, I messed about trying to keep the boat sailing. In the early afternoon I gave it up and had a snooze. A French yacht passed on more or less the same course motoring at slow speed and making good progress. I didn't have much fuel and I was unhappy about capitulating immediately and motoring. That didn't seem to fit in with the new way of life either. In the evening some cloud began to build from the west and it looked as if I might get sailing again, and I did for a while, but it didn't last so I dropped the main and rolled away the jib to stop the boat.

The lights of an aircraft heading south twinkled above. I thought of the passengers sipping their drinks and settling down to their movies, little knowing that a few thousand feet below, a solitary Scot sat in a small boat waiting for a breeze.

With the lights on the mast reflecting in the still water I lay down on the starboard bunk fully clothed and ready for anything. Eventually I went to sleep.

At daybreak the next morning the wind came away fresh on the starboard side. Good to be moving but I was gradually being pushed to the east and couldn't lay Cabo Prior. So rather than prolong the trip and beat out to the west I abandoned the idea of going to La Coruna and headed to Viviero, anchoring off the breakwater just after first light. It all looked very clean and fresh in the morning sun. I was pretty pleased with myself, ate some breakfast and went to sleep, peacefully at rest in my first real foreign port of the trip. The peace lasted until noon when noise from the anchor chain woke me and I found Beyond dragging towards the sea wall. Engine on, up anchor fast and motor into the harbour was the course of action. Perhaps marinas weren't that bad after all.

Viviero was somewhere between a fishing village and a small seaside town and very much off the tourist trail. People seemed to speak neither French nor much English but despite my lack of Spanish I managed to get some laundry done and buy a small cooking pot. I felt no real need to learn any Spanish on the basis that I wouldn't be there for long and, anyway, I was hoping that things would probably become much easier as I headed south.

After a couple of days I set off again, beating round Cape Ortegal, marvelling at the vandalism carried out in the name of progress with the once beautiful headland strewn with disfiguring wind turbines. It might be a good way of generating clean energy but what a price to pay. The great majority of the population probably never appreciate the extent of the visual damage caused by wind farms. The full effect is only appreciated when you are at sea and I hate wind turbines. To me they represent the unstoppable power of governments who decide what's best for people without any thought for the damage they are doing to a once beautiful landscape. But that's progress I suppose.

I anchored in the bay at Cedeira, surrounded by green hills and the next day encountered another stiff beat round to Coruna. These headlands were tough going with a big swell and strong tides, reminding me back home of Ardnamurchan.

Coruna was a good, if expensive shelter, but I found the town unappealing and a bit grubby. When I get tired

I become impatient with things that don't at first appeal and often find myself forming negative first impressions about places. Thankfully, things always look better after a good meal and a sleep. Over the next few days I worked my way south, anchoring first at Ares then Mara continuing to sail fast in a strong northeasterly wind into Camarinas where, when I finally got the anchor to hold, I rested for a few days enjoying the peace. Annoyingly, worries about not working were still there and it wasn't easy to relax properly but I hoped things would get better.

It was now September and, as the new month arrived, I made my way further south, rounding Finisterre and anchoring in Sardiniera. Before I left my home I had told my sailing friends that they would be more than welcome on any stage of the trip which was very big-hearted of me since I didn't even know for sure where I was headed. But, as they say, it's the thought that counts. Only one person had taken me up on the offer and she was heading down to Bayonna to meet the boat so I had to do my best to get there. I had only been away a matter of weeks but I was looking forward to meeting someone from home. Perhaps the life of the lone rover wasn't for me after all. I worked my way steadily down the coast from beautiful bay to bay, day sailing, anchoring in the evenings and feeling pretty pleased with myself. The coast is stunning and the bays are a bit like Scottish lochs with their pine-covered hills and beaches but that was where the similarity ended. Here the sun shone.But I felt I was getting on okay. I hadn't made any serious mistakes, there had been no real problems, I was eating well, and it was warm. Some of my disquiet about not working seemed to be fading and I found myself thinking just a little less about it. But it was early days. On the way round the coast I had met up with another couple of yachts and we had become friendly, sharing evening drinks. The cruising life was finally turning out to be a little more sociable. Things came to a head in Portosin, when, after an extended and very liquid lunch, I phoned my old office in Korea. They told me later that I talked nonsense for about ten minutes and concluded by asking them if they would all like to come over to Spain - rather a long way they thought. Perhaps it was just as well that I had retired when I did.

Further south I anchored at the Islas Ceis where it was mountainous, wooded and beautiful. The three islands form a nature reserve and I later learned that I should have had a permit to visit them but there were so many boats there that I doubt if anyone was bothered. After a peaceful night at anchor I headed into Bayonna. A couple of the boats I had met further up the coast were there already and I watched as another arrived. We ignored the marina's instructions and found a space where the three of us could be side by side and by early evening we were in fine form. I had completely forgotten that my new crew member, Christine, was due to arrive from Glasgow and when she did she must have wondered what she had walked into. It's always difficult to join a party when everyone else has reached flying speed hours ago but she entered into the spirit of the occasion and we all got along fine.

One evening we slipped into Leixoes and anchored in the shelter of the breakwater arm. My cruise almost ended there when I tried to ignite a disposable barbeque on the stern. It had been aboard for a while and had dried up so, after a couple of failed attempts, I put a little outboard petrol on it and tried again and it lit alright. What seemed like a towering inferno shot skyward and began to spread. I was worried about my lovely teak until I realised the thing was sitting on top of the locker holding the gas bottles. Losing some eyebrow in the process, I managed to get it over the side and we settled for a steak pie cooked in the oven. We were sitting digesting our meal when there was a muffled explosion which shook the boat and made the pots and pans jump and rattle in their locker below the galley stove. What next? It turned out workmen were constructing a new passenger terminal and blasting underwater. I had had enough and the next morning we slipped into the inner harbour and I thought to hell with the expense. Over the next week we made our way down the coast of Portugal to Nazare where Christine left to return to work in Scotland and I headed on to Lisbon, then to Lagos, to carry on with what was becoming a highly enjoyable new life.

3

Portugal to the Cape Verdes

Off to the west

AFTER two days in Lisbon I slipped out and headed further down the coast, rounding Cape St. Vincent and sailing into Lagos where I stayed for ten days. It was expensive but worth it to get a few jobs done on the boat. I wanted to get some sort of crutch arrangement for the boom because even heading into the sea and swell, when I lowered the main, the boom would swing from side to side much more than was safe if I was up on the coach roof trying to get a couple of sail ties round it. So I got the boatyard to make up a low fame onto which I was going to slot a vertical tube with a crutch on the top of it. It cost a lot and rather disfigured the boat and the crutch idea was never really successful but it also gave me something solid to hold onto between leaving the safety of the cockpit and getting to the shrouds, which previously had been the closest thing I was able to hang onto. I was having problems with the alternator as well. The engine would start perfectly but the alternator often failed to start charging. The fault lay in the engine start panel, which like the rest of the engine was over 20 years old and looked pretty rough. I had made various attempts to repair it and thought about getting an entirely new panel until I found what one would cost. So I bodged it up again with the help of a local guy, who seemed to know what he was talking about, and carried on. My daughter, Anna, came down for a few days and we went round the coast to the famous grottoes to swim in the deep blue Atlantic water.

I was planning to head over to Porto Santo then go on to Madeira. Another sailor from Scotland was due to arrive for the trip over which I hoped would take about five days. I hadn't known George long but he was a friend of another sailing friend and wanted to get some sea miles in. Some rough weather went through and once things had died down a bit, and the weather maps showed that there was a reasonable spell coming, we set off. There was still a big swell running, but the wind was a helpful force four from the northwest and, for the first two days things went well, although the wind shifted and we started beating into it. On the morning of the third day the barometer dropped a few millibars and it was clear that there was a front on its way. Things started getting squally, making life uncomfortable even with two reefs in and only a small headsail up. The glass continued to fall and by evening I dropped the headsail and let the boat sit at about fifty degrees to the wind with three reefs in the main. We were perfectly safe but it was very rough, wet and pretty cold. George, who is an ex-infantry soldier, was turning out to be just the kind of guy to have on board on nights like this having been trained to put up with just about anything. Nothing seemed to bother him so I was a little concerned when I went below in the middle of a particularly wild hour to see him reading a small well-thumbed bible. However, he assured me it was something he did every day and no reflection on his confidence in me. I emailed one of my sailing pals ashore whom I knew would be watching our progress and the weather and asked him what he thought. Back came the encouraging reply: "Better for a while after this front, but more shit on Friday,"- nothing like having a positive attitude.

In the next 24 hours another front came and we passed under it beneath a dark and dramatic sky, the wind shifting yet again. I was quite used to this sort of thing and wasn't worried, only irritated by the discomfort, but despite being new to it George carried on as usual. At one stage he managed to bake a couple of baguettes in the oven, sitting on the cabin sole in his lifejacket, opening the oven door as the stove swung away from him to check progress, then slamming it shut again before the boat rolled the other way and our bread shot out. What a guy. The hot bread tasted great. Things stayed pretty wild for a while, then as the barometer steadied up, gradually eased to the point where I was able to go forward and set the storm jib. The boat took off and started to make real progress arriving in Porto Santo one morning five days out from Lagos. We were both whacked and there was a big swell running into the marina but we managed to secure the boat with lots of fenders and an anchor hung in the middle of one of the headlines to quieten the motion.

Later that afternoon after lunch, and a couple of safe arrival whiskies, I went for a nap intending to go ashore in the evening but I didn't make it and stayed in my bunk until the next morning. A few of the boats, which had been on swinging moorings in the harbour, had suffered problems because of the swell driven by the weather. One had been damaged and another arrived next day having come from the Mediterranean via Gibraltar, suffering the same passage of wild stuff that we had experienced.

George headed home, my weather forecasting chum, Jerry, arrived and we sailed over to Quinton de Lorde, a small artificial harbour on Madeira.

The marina at Quinto De Lorde had rather a surreal atmosphere. It was the centrepiece of what had been planned as an exclusive holiday apartment complex but the development had fallen victim to the recession now gripping Europe and all work had come to a halt. There was a very smart site office complete with an elaborate model of how things would be if it were all finished and a very glamorous and immaculately-clad lady trying not to look bored as day after day she waited in vain for the prospective buyers who never came. Many of the buildings had facades only and no roofs. It was very much like a film set where the appearance only mattered from a certain angle. But the marina staff were very friendly and helpful and, despite the cost, it was a pleasure to be there. Most of the new cruising friends I had met on the Spanish and Portuguese coasts were still stuck in the Algarve, heading off on rallies to various destinations or returning to the UK to replenish funds. I felt a bit like the Lone Ranger but I couldn't hang around any longer. I had come 1600 miles since leaving Falmouth and I was growing in confidence every day but the budget was starting to creak and it seemed like time to get going again.

A friend from another British boat had taken pity on my complete ineptitude on all matters related to IT and had helped me through the process of downloading an Internet weather file viewer and getting myself registered as a user. So I triumphantly downloaded a Grib file via the satellite phone, barely managing to restrain myself from doing lap of honour of the pontoons to celebrate my new-found skill. I am not a Luddite but I am slow to adopt new things and it was only two years since I had fitted my first headsail furler and bought a plotter. I still remember how impressed I was with them when, after retiring with boat problems from a single-handed race halfway from Kinsale to Santander, I found myself running for shelter into Camaret in a gale with driving rain and practically no visibility. I had only to glance down through the hatch at the plotter screen to see exactly where I was and furl in more or less headsail to keep perfect control. I felt like a caveman who had just been shown an electric light.

But back to the present - The Pilot book assured me I would enjoy following winds and a favourable current and, although the weather looked very light for the next 36 hours, it was predicted to go into the northeast after that, so I slipped the lines and headed out, feeling that even a slow passage would at least get me a bit further down the line and stop the cash register clinking. Nights at sea were still, for the time being, free.

Outside there was just enough wind to sail with so figuring I would be better making some progress, even if it was slow, I disregarded the call of the anchorage and headed roughly for Graciosa, or as near to the course as the light wind and swell would allow. With an apparent wind of about eight knots, right on the nose, we began to amble more or less towards the Canaries. Having to sail high for pressure there was, though, much more east in the course than I would have wanted.

Trying to get back into a sensible seagoing routine after a week of socialising, I bravely held out until happy hour before cracking a beer and, feeling very virtuous, crawled slowly past Islas Desertas in the gathering cloudless dusk.

The almost full pure silver moon killed all but the brightest stars and the Man in the Moon was wearing Mars hung at navel height like a disco medallion. I had enough fresh stuff for three nights, plenty of water and a big supply of packets, so the domestic side things looked optimistic. I cleaned a couple of calamari and fried them in onion rings with lime, beautiful. It was the good life indeed.

For a few hours we slid along under the stars with the boat seeming to get enough power to keep going from virtually no apparent wind but eventually the swell prevailed and she wouldn't stay on course any longer. By nine there was no wind to sail with and I stowed the sails and lashed the boom. Setting the AIS and Sea Me as electronic guardians and, with a one hour interval on the timer, I lay down for the first night at sea as the boat rolled gently in the swell and the various jars and bottles clinked and rumbled in the lockers. On an hourly basis the alarm sounded its call to arms and I checked around but no change, still a lovely night. Grand for romance but not much good for the solo sailor who would, for the time being at least, prefer a little wind.

Up and about at eight I got the boat underway, first courtesy of Dr. Diesel, whilst I dispatched the last of the Madeira sausages. Then, as the sun got up, a light breeze came through and we spent the day ghosting from one patch of wind to the other whilst the sun beat down. At noon we had covered 77 miles since leaving the marina, surprisingly good, I felt. Still, the Portuguese Trades were clearly taking the day off.

The same daily pattern repeated itself. By eight in the evening we had done all we could, even trying to sail low with the asymmetric but it made little impression. As the moon made its appearance, and the sun disappeared for the day, so did even the little wind we had enjoyed and it was time to snug her down and settle in for another night of relatively gentle rolling under the stars. But no sooner had I dropped the main, than the day played its last card. A light south-easterly came up and we slid along under the moon until about one in the morning when progress came to halt again.

Next morning, after an hour of motoring to charge, I got the boat going, initially on a southerly heading, but the wind veered as the morning went on and I tacked onto starboard, enjoying some good sailing in nearly flat water with the monitor doing its stuff and the boat sailing to its numbers. *Beyond* is not a light boat but she goes surprising well in light stuff, the key number being ten forty five, standing for ten knots apparent wind, forty degrees on the bow and five knots of boat speed. We bettered it consistently. I always find that the less you try and sail the boat the better she goes. The monitor seems to have just the right touch, particularly with the lines a little slack. In the puffs the boat starts to sail a little high and feeds on the increasing apparent wind she creates for herself, boat speed and angle climbing, until she is at optimum. Then as the puff goes through and the breeze reverts she bears away, and slows, until the next puff when the process begins anew. It's a pleasure to watch and I let her get on with it. Mid-morning a loaded bulker went by heading north but, apart from that, there was nothing to see. The sun beat down, the sea was incredibly blue and, with the cockpit temperature in the high thirties, I didn't spend much time outside. Using the sprayhood as a sunshade was a new experience for me. It was a big change from the West of Scotland and I enjoyed it.

We had a good day's sail with a steadier and slightly stronger breeze thankfully still ahead so, although the true speed wasn't up to much, with careful trimming the apparent pressure was good enough to get us up around six knots at times and the sunshine did the rest. Evening brought a sky that would have delighted shepherds the world over and a slight wind shift into the west.

It seemed to get dark really early and, with lights on, the friendly moon again beamed down on us. *Beyond* slid along whilst I toasted the evening in the now cool breeze that was blowing across the boat. The fridge was starting to look a little bare and struggling in the hot weather but I concocted a stir fry with some chicken leftovers, the last leek, some broccoli and an onion. Thank God for the onions as they seemed to keep forever.

Stopped and drifting again by midnight. With just thirty miles to go, I took the building cirrus cloud up high to mean there might be a little more energy available the next day and felt optimistic. Sure enough by four the next morning there was a light westerly and we got going again. As the sun crawled over the horizon at eight, the shapes of the outlying Canary Islands began to emerge from the gloom.

By late morning we rounded the south tip of Graciosa and sailed past the anchorage at Playa Francesca packed with boats of all nationalities. Eagerly anticipating a cold shower, and the chance to eat some fresh food, I motored north into the marina at Caleta del Sebo, where a frantically waving and shouting official on the harbour wall told me I was not permitted to enter and directed me to "Go to the beach."

It seemed my clearance from Madeira was insufficient and that a particular pass was required to berth in the harbour. Now I began to understand why the anchorage was so busy. They weren't all purists after all, or Scots like me trying to avoid paying marina dues. They were the great unwanted, the turning away of whom clearly kept the gent on the harbour wall in a steady job. So I avoided the crowd and anchored in the bay just south of the marina, along with one other boat, which, I assumed, had, like me, come along too late to find a space amongst the main body of the international cruising brotherhood. We formed a small but growing gathering as other boats, excluded from the harbour, joined us as the day wore on. The sun shone and late in the afternoon the breeze I could so well have done with on the way over, finally filled in and blew hard for a couple of days. The anchor held steady and she dug in and sat sweetly even in the hardest gusts.

It had been a slow trip; 300 miles in four days was hardly record-breaking but I had enjoyed it and, although I was still in Europe, Scotland seemed far enough away to make me feel that I was truly voyaging.

I had a good day's sail down the west coast of Lanzarote in big waves and very strong wind in the acceleration zone at the corner and berthed in Marina Rubicon, Playa Blanca, one of the most pleasant marinas I had ever been in. It was an immaculate place, really well run, very helpful staff, swimming pools, restaurants, supermarkets, doctors, everything and all for 23 euros a night. The bar walls were adorned with signed photographs of many of the greats of ocean sailing to give the place an air of authenticity, although the lady behind the bar had no idea who any of them were, and certainly had never seen any of them in her bar. But it was place to enjoy and I certainly did. I also took the opportunity to haul the boat out and take a look at the anti-fouling and the anodes, both of which I renewed, rubbing down the bottom and changing from the Teflon based racing stuff I had put on at the start of the season to a cruising spec and putting on plenty of it. As a consequence the bottom of the boat changed from being white to dark blue which somehow it seemed appropriate for her new role.

I left Rubicon and spent a few days at anchor then went down to Fuertaventura to a couple of anchorages before crossing the 120 miles to Tenerife. Fuerteventura was fairly routine, except for the fact that I met John Woolfe and his partner, Wendy, who were on the way back to Wellington in New Zealand after six years of wandering around the world.

John came over one afternoon introduced himself and told me that his boat, a steel Roberts design, was also called *Beyond*. Not only that, he seemed to take the view that I should change the name of mine. Ho ho. Once the initial name thing had been put to one side we got on pretty well and, as the months went by and the two boats met up frequently, we became good mates.

I moved on to Santa Cruz, Tenerife. The marina was full of boats getting ready to cross to the Caribbean with lots of dreamers wandering around looking for crewing jobs. I got fed up with the same guys coming by every day and asking me if I needed crew. They had clearly asked so many boats that they could no longer distinguish one from the other. I had to laugh when they arrived one morning and walked towards *Beyond* then recognised me and did an about-turn. They seemed to have finally got the message. There were lots of notices taped to the harbour gates advertising crew availability.

One of the ads actually said: "Hello! I am a Mexican musician. I have not sailed but I dream of going to Brazil." That's all you need, isn't it? Some guy in a big hat spewing all day and playing with his maracas.

The wheel had developed a bit of fore and aft play where it joined the pedestal and I had planned to replace the top bearings in Tenerife. When I finally got the old ones out I found the spares I had been sent were the wrong size.

It turned out that the ones for my boat had been sent to New Zealand and I had the ones that should have been down there. Much hassle, many taxi rides, Euros, phone calls and several days later I had it sorted out. I finally left and anchored overnight in a bay to the south of the island to get myself organised. There was bad weather coming in about four days and I wanted to get south as soon as possible, both to avoid that and to steer well clear of the massed madness of the Arc, due to leave Las Palmas within a couple of days.

But next morning when I started the engine there was no flow of cooling water so I drifted out from the land, tried various things and eventually swapped impellers, which solved the problem. What with the steering bearings, the starter panel and the impeller I was getting pretty good at taking things to bits. Later in the morning the breeze came in and I was off towards Cape Verde Islands where I had arranged to meet up with one of the old racing crew, James, who was flying out from UK, laden with charts, various strange bits for the boat, tea bags, and a couple of Fray Bentos steak pies.

The trade winds were on holiday again, although the wind was forward of the beam, completely the opposite to the seasonal prediction. I had a great passage towards the Cape Verdes with one windy night when I was reefed but, generally, it was warm, flattish water sailing and I managed two full six hour spells of sleep when the Sea Me had no ships to warn me about. I managed 360 miles in the first 48 hours and the days were warm and sunny. The boat sailed on, the monitor steered and with plenty to eat and a couple of cold beers at happy hour, what more could I ask?

I caught my first fish but I threw it back because I had just made my tea and I couldn't see the point in killing it. It was about two feet long, greenish yellow, with spots down its sides and an unhappy expression on its face. At one stage I had some sort of vague idea that I would be catching and eating lots of fish and living the life of a true ocean nomad. In Falmouth I had bought a second-hand deep sea reel, some line and a few lures. But either I was using the wrong lures, or going too fast, or maybe too slow or perhaps I was just no good as a fisherman because the only fish I had eaten so far were from a tin.

I arrived in Palmeira in the Cape Verdes after seven days of easy sailing and squeezed into the crowded anchorage. It was stinking hot and by the ramshackle stone quay there were a few very broken-down looking houses and a couple of boarded up bars. The dogs wandering about looked starved and the whole place had a sad air of poverty about it but there was a shack selling cold beer and the people were very friendly so I settled in to wait for James. Two days later we sailed to Mindelo, the main port in the islands.

Things were easy in Mindelo. Customs and Immigration officers were some of the friendliest and helpful I had ever come across, although mooring stern on in the marina was something of a problem with the wind vane hanging off the stern. Although bits of the waterfront have been developed and there is a very smart marina office with tight security, you only had to cross the main road and walk the quiet and poorly lit streets to sense that the buildings crowded together there had an atmosphere all of their own.

In the evening locals and visiting sailors headed for the bar across the road to listen to local musicians, drink ice cold beer from tall frosty bottles and mix with the stunning local girls who would wander in and out. Not being allowed into the marina, the girls would wait outside the gate, fall into step beside you, take your hand and do their best to lead you to the land of plenty. I could happily have stayed longer but we had an ocean to cross and, after a few days, we said our farewells to the other sailors we had met and headed off for Barbados

4

Across the
Atlantic

Two Men in a Boat

WE left Mindelo on the morning of Saturday, December 4 at about ten motoring out into the bay. For the first few hours the wind which funnels between the islands kept going. But as the day wore on we started to lose the breeze and had to do some motoring through the night. By day two, though, things got into a pattern and we sailed along nicely with the wind behind. Each morning at about seven the sun rose behind us and worked its way overhead and by late morning it was hot with a few small clouds and a very blue sea. We would run the engine for an hour or so to recharge the batteries and switch the fridge on, which we only ran along with the engine. Thankfully, the sun slid behind the mainsail by the early afternoon and we could enjoy some shade in the cockpit. The wind blew and the boat sailed on with the monitor steering and the off-duty guy snoozing in the shade below.

We worked three hour watches, with two dog watches between noon and three so that the rota changed and we got alternate days of each watch. At noon we recorded the position and the miles run from the previous day, usually about 130, and the miles to go to our destination. By late afternoon the off-watch guy would start to get the evening meal ready and, more importantly, made sure there were a couple of cold beers ready for happy hour which we enjoyed just before sundown. There was a strict ration of two beers each, or one beer and a glass of wine, usually with some nuts or crisps. Since that's the only alcohol we allowed ourselves we really looked forward to it. About this time each day we would send off our emails via the satellite phone and receive any incoming messages as well as the three day look ahead for the weather.

With so little cloud the horizon was hard and clear, and by seven in the evening the sun would hit the edge of our little world and you could almost hear it sizzle to announce the close of day. With hardly any twilight it was dark before seven and, with no moon, the stars were all out on parade. I enjoyed renewing old acquaintances from my seafaring days with stately Orion rising behind us keeping a fatherly eye on our progress.

By eight dinner is over, the galley wiped down and the boat in quiet mode. One of us is in the cockpit keeping an eye on things while the other is fast asleep. In the good weather, with no spray, we kept the hatches open and as the boat cooled down the air flowing through the cabin made sleeping a pleasure. But when it was blowing we had to close up the forward hatch and things got a bit sweaty.

And so the nights wore on, three hours on and three off, reeling in the miles with the stars climbing from behind us and heading towards the west horizon providing reassuring proof that the world was still turning. Even with the rough and sweaty bits we seemed to be having better conditions than those at home. We heard via the emails of snow, ice and the usual chaos which seems to strike every year at the first sign of winter weather

We ate very well with some fresh food from Mindelo providing the basis for the meals for the first three days out. The potatoes, carrots and onions kept well and we had lots of eggs and so far we had not had to dig too deeply into the large stock of tinned stuff we kept in reserve. Pre-baked baguettes were also a success and went down well stuffed with some tinned fish. We were on Long Life milk, which I quite enjoy, with a carton lasting a couple of days. The boat stayed dry and clean. It was a pleasure to be aboard and a double pleasure for me to have someone else with whom to share the day-to-day routines, particularly James. We had been racing boats together off and on for ten years and had some great memories, as well as the same tastes in food and drink and sense of humour.

Things changed about five days out as it became windy and very rough with a big swell and we reduced sail. But we were comfortable enough and making a good speed without too much strain on the boat. I liked to keep it that way because there was a long way to go. Then one night it got really wild with rain squalls and a very big sea coming up behind. We reduced sail more and more and by one in the morning when things got particularly wild, I had to shout up James, who was sleeping below, and between us we got the mainsail down and the boom lashed which was a big improvement.

That left us with just the small headsail up but even so we were still tearing along at eight knots, rolling about a lot and having to hang on tight down below. Big waves rolled past the boat and the stars disappeared behind the rain clouds as the squalls went by. Nearly all my solo ocean and offshore racing had been on the wind. This was the longest spell I had spent running. When you are racing you have to push the boat to get speed and stay in the hunt but not push so hard that you either break something or get so tired that you can't function properly. Now I could take it easy, keep the strain on the boat and ourselves to a minimum and not worry about losing a knot. James, on the other hand, revelled in the conditions and would take the boat off the wind vane and steer by hand, surfing down the waves in the dark and loving it. On more than one occasion I would awaken feeling the boat surging along with her stern lifting and shout "James!" We're going too fast." It became a standing joke between us. The sea was really confusing, the kind of thing you get in the Irish Sea or on the west coast of Scotland when the tide is running into the wind, not what you would expect out there in the open ocean. It prevented the boat from finding a rhythm making life below difficult and we had to be careful to avoid injury, especially when cooking. It would have been easy to fall or get flung across the cabin and sustain an injury.

But in mileage terms we were making good, if jerky, progress. Then things settled down a bit as the unpleasant band of squally weather had gone through, and we were back in the sun, but still rolling quite a lot. We set the twin headsails and were doing okay at that. After all these years of seeing pictures of yachts rolling down the trades with their twin headsails set, I was finally doing it in my own boat and it felt good.

At noon today, Saturday, December 11, there were 1007 miles behind us and 1070 more to go and we passed the halfway mark, round about happy hour, strangely enough.

We had a bit of a fright one day when I discovered that a six pack of Portuguese beer contained five punctured cans and I was concerned that more of our stock might have suffered the same fate. It seemed that alloy cans had to be kept absolutely still in the locker as the constant rubbing of any motion soon punctured their thin edges. I re-stowed the rest of the stock on a towel inside the locker. I was learning. We took the small number four off the stay and put up the new running sail, twinned with the genoa, which worked really well since the sails are made to match each other and there's an even balance on each side of the bow. For a couple of days we enjoyed lovely sailing. The sea settled down, the twins pulled the boat along, the monitor steered and the miles rolled by under the keel. This was easy on the crew and the boat; easy to cook. Easy to sleep and dream, to be sure.

Whoever was off-watch from three till six in the afternoon decided on the time of happy hour and served the drinks, usually with some ceremony, and presented the nibble of the day. As the second week wore on our choice of snacks grew pretty limited and hit a low when I announced that, in recognition of the boat's Scottish connections, the snack of the day was porridge oats and handed up a bowl of them. James wasn't sure whether I was joking or not but looked relieved when I produced a bowl of olives. We did try a couple of oats each but they were too dry.

Spinning out our one glass of cold San Miguel became something of an art. I have never been a sipper when it comes to beer and it wasn't easy. However, I remembered reading about survivors in rafts who would hold a sip of water in their mouths for as long as they could, before swallowing it, and I adopted that technique. Who knows? I may yet become one of those guys who can sit in the pub and make a pint last half an hour but then again perhaps not.

Meanwhile, the miles rolled by and we altered course and planned to make the best of the apparent angles.

My earlier scorn of the Grib File culture had completely evaporated and I began to look forward to getting a fresh set to see what we might expect over the coming days. They turned out to be very accurate in terms of strength and direction and let us plan ahead, in terms of whether we went south or north of the line. There's no point in trying to sail dead downwind in the light winds. With the swell astern we just wound up rolling and flapping at slow speed so we usually sailed high on whatever was the making gybe and waited for a shift.

I always put in a series of intermediate waypoints into the system which give an early indication of whether or not you are getting off the line. If you only put in one, which might be over a thousand miles away, you can be way off line before the bearing to waypoint changes even by a couple of degrees. Intermediate waypoints also made good psychological stepping stones. As the week wore on and we got closer the miles to go readout on the cockpit repeater marked our progress until, with only a few hundred left to go, we felt as if we were almost there. Thoughts of what we would do in Barbados began to occupy our minds - unrationed consumption of cold beers and a meal ashore seemed high on the list of priorities.

At noon on Saturday 18 we had just 120 miles to go and the weather was fresh on the starboard quarter with a steep swell running under the boat making it tough to get down to the final waypoint, just south of the island. By midnight we had two reefs in the main and much of the jib rolled away. At two on Sunday morning I altered course to pass north of the island instead, preferring to do the slight extra distance for the sake of getting into some flatter water sooner. There was no doubt about it; we were getting tired. It worked well and James raised the lights of the island at about five in the morning as we tore along in the rain squalls. At seven, when I was on watch, the monitor line to the wheel parted where it went through the turning block. It went with a bang and I grabbed the wheel as the boat shot up into the wind. I tried the auto pilot but it kept letting the boat run up to starboard. I managed to replace the monitor line with a short length cut from the tail of the boom guy by steering with my knees whilst cutting and tying. I felt pretty pleased with myself, multi-tasking to be sure.

There was another boat ahead of us appearing and disappearing in the rain and we heard them calling the port on VHF. We rounded the top end of the island and turned south gradually getting out of the swell. We sailed close in under the coast towards Bridgetown. Port control instructed us to go right up into the main harbour where we were to moor and get clearance and we got everything down and motored in. It was very hot and with the various problems that had arisen I was feeling pretty frazzled and very glad not to be on my own.

We motored past a couple of cruise ships, moored alongside, but when we got to the head of the harbour the residual swell running in was being bounced back as it hit the dead end of the concrete wall and you could see that there was dangerous motion. The boat that had been just ahead of us on the way down had already tied alongside and the crew shouted a warning as the boat bounced backwards and forwards against the big hard, vertical sprung fendering - no doubt ideal for a cruise ship but hopeless for a yacht. If I had been thinking straight and not so tired I would have headed back out, gone to the bay and anchored but I wasn't and we decided to have a go. We circled a couple of times to pick a spot and managed to get our own fenders lined up against one fender pad, and lassoo a bollard about amidships. An elderly gent on a pushbike wearing a fluorescent waistcoat cycled up and told us his job was docking ships. We threw him a headline which he strolled off with and eventually managed to secure to a bollard.

I jumped ashore, which was a challenge in itself, and headed to the office with the boat papers leaving James to cope with the surge, alternately fending off manually and working the engine to keep the fenders lined up. With the business done I headed back as quickly as I could and, picking a moment when the boat came in close to the fendering, I jumped aboard. We got out as fast as possible and headed round into Carlisle Bay where we anchored early in the afternoon in turquoise water over silver sand.

I had a few cans of McEwan's Export which had been stashed away since I left UK. Earlier in the day I had managed to sneak them into the fridge without James knowing. I produced them with a flourish and we sat in the cockpit, taking in our surroundings, and slowly began to unwind.

It was a very, very happy hour indeed.

5

Welcome to Barbados

And have a nice day . . .

ANCHORED off the jetty In Carlisle Bay the wind blew and the swell rolled in. Access to the shore was either via the jetty at 'The Boatyard', a beach bar just along the shore. The alternative was a long outboard trip to the north into the river to land at the careenage below the town. At the boatyard incoming crew members were required to pay a standing charge of $20 Barbados per person to land at the jetty and you had to wear a wristband to show that you had paid. You could redeem that if you bought food at the bar. So, in effect, you could land at the jetty but you have to spend $20 dollars at the bar to do so. My first suspicion that Bridgetown thrived by fleecing the visitor was beginning to dawn.

Bridgetown may well be a historic part of Barbadian culture. I am sure it isn't representative of the island, which I believe is a mass of up-market golf courses and hotels but it seemed to me to have had its day. Like so many places whose prosperity depends on the cruise ship industry, it appeared to have surrendered to the commercial pressures of the duty-free world where globalisation has completely wrecked any trace of genuine history. Around the centre, diamond dealers, designer shops and duty free jewellers did their best to tempt the visitor to spend. A block away the real world carried on its day-to-day business amongst boarded-up shops, broken windows and grubby supermarkets catering to the everyday needs of the locals.

One day there were five large cruise ships in the harbour at the same time and probably about 10,000 visitors in circulation. Some of the more elderly passengers looked pale and bewildered and seemed to prefer to cling to the security of the terminal building itself rather than risk venturing into the throng ashore. Others, clearly veterans of the cruising life, queued for taxis and headed off to shop.

Quite apart from the shipped-in visitors with their dollars and plastic, the town was in full grip of the pre-Christmas spending spree. One day I stood in line for over half an hour in a market to get to the check out. The atmosphere was friendly enough and when some very big guys just pushed their way to the front with a case of beer on each shoulder, no one seemed inclined to object, and I certainly didn't want to start a riot. In amongst it all the locals, particularly the older ladies, seemed to maintain a certain quiet dignity dressed in their flowered hats, Sunday best dresses and courtly manners. They must sometimes wonder what has happened to their town.

On cruise ship days the atmosphere at 'The Boatyard' bar was a frantic mixture of sun, sand and alcohol-fuelled lunacy. I got the impression that the younger members of the cruise ship set and some who could vaguely remember having once being younger, had been bussed straight from the terminal to the bar. The sunshine, beach and blasting reggae music provided the basic ingredients of a good time with industrial quantities of drink completing the job.

As the afternoon wore on the scene began to resemble Robbie Burns' account of the witches' dance at Kirk Alloway. At one stage as the music blared, the barman walked along the top of the bar with a bottle in each hand blowing on a referee's whistle and pouring neat drink straight down the throats of his adoring, bikinied, pierced and tattooed customers, crowding to get to the front and gain his attention. Their heads were craned back like baby birds in the nest when mother has brought home a particularly tasty worm.

Eventually, as the afternoon wore on the buses arrived and the bemused congregation stumbled and dribbled their way back to whichever ship they had arrived on, ready to sail onwards to the next authentic Caribbean experience. Perhaps I was just getting old.

Further down the bay, the Barbados Yacht Club offered a more subdued welcome. I presented my credentials as a wandering Scot, surrendered my Visa card, and was granted temporary membership and issued with a code against which I could charge food and drink. I felt at home and immediately tested the system by buying a steak and a couple of cold beers before joining the family groups around the bar and buffet; civilisation at last.

James had headed home to join his family for Christmas and I spent the day alone at anchor. The swell was rolling in and it was too rough to land at the jetty so I anchored the dinghy off the beach and swam in hoping, I recall, to find someone to talk to. I bought a beer at the shanty and sat down gratefully on a lounger. "Where's your ticket, Mon?"said a voice. "I don't have one. I just bought a beer," I replied. "Well, you need a ticket to sit on a lounger and beer and loungers is separate, Mon," he said. Happy Christmas.

At night, the beach bars got going around ten or eleven and the music blasted and reverberated right across the bay, usually until about four or five the next morning. There was no escape from the racket. For someone who was basically dead tired and just wanted to sleep, it was a complete pain. The night before I left, John and Wendy arrived on the other *Beyond* and we had a good re- union.

My final Barbados experience pretty much summed the place up for me. Eager to clear outwards and get away to Grenada, I had walked along the shore to the passenger terminal where the Customs and Immigration offices were located. Since everything had to be done in stages, I had been to the office where the fees were paid and handed over my $100 for my outward clearance in return for a slip acknowledging that I had paid. I then visited Immigration to have my crew list checked. Only the Customs formalities remained as the final hurdle.

I joined the queue of yachties waiting patiently outside the 'Great Man's' office for their turn to present their documentation and get formal permission to leave. One crew complained that they had been there for an hour already.

My turn came and I entered the office where an immaculately-clad figure wearing epaulettes sat silently behind the desk with the air of someone posing for a portrait. I was motioned to sit, which I did in the most respectful manner I could muster, laying out my various papers on the desk. Each was inspected in silence with a degree of concentration worthy of a pathologist carefully considering some vital piece of forensic evidence under a microscope. Finally, the last piece of paper was laid aside without any having received the blessing of the official stamp. I began to worry. Finally, the man looked up and spoke. "Now", he said with a charming smile, "'I would like you go and get me some cigarettes". Under the circumstances there didn't seem much point in arguing, but I pointed out that I had just spent $100 on my clearance and that I was close to broke.

"No, no," he said looking horrified. "I will give you the money, captain. Please take your passport to the duty-free shop at the arrivals hall and bring me four cartons of Bensons, the ones in the gold wrapper and when you get back your clearance will be ready." He produced a wad of notes that would have choked a donkeyand carelessly peeled off a few.

Off I scuttled to join the throng of tourists eager to be parted with their dollars, bought the cigarettes and returned to the office just as the next patient crew were being ushered in, only to be ushered out again the moment I arrived. If looks could have killed,

"Ah, captain, come in, come in. Close the door please. Thank you. Please be seated," he said. I handed over the loot and was given my ship's papers back plus the all-important clearance signed and stamped.

I was free to go.

"Have a pleasant voyage, captain," he said.

"You too, your honour,"

A SHORT DASH TO GRENADA

I sailed over to Grenada, a rough overnight trip, during which the drum holding the wind vane lines started to part company with the wheel. At first, when the boat started shearing about in the dark, it was hard to see what had happened so I disconnected the vane and spent six hours on the wheel hand steering in very gusty weather. I was glad to get into Prickly Bay. The next day I took the wheel ashore and had the drum welded on to it. It was the first of quite a few modifications I would make to the steering gear.

I had never made a passage on a yacht in hot weather like this before and leaving Europe I had naively thought that I could just power the fridge by running the engine for a while each day. But a couple of days out from Barbados I had found a few maggots in the bottom of the fridge and they didn't even look cold. I bought a solar panel and that made a huge difference as it happily charged away as long as the sun shone keeping the use of the engine to a minimum.

The engine itself was starting to show signs that its 20 years of intermittent work had taken their toll. Although it never failed to start, quite a few small things had started to go wrong, and in Barbados the water pump casing had cracked, leaking raw salt water. I hung an empty soup can under it but you could only run it for about five minutes before the can was full and the excess water landed on the alternator belt and got sprayed around. I contacted the dealer in St Lucia hoping to get a replacement. The old problem with the alternator was still there, despite trying a number of dodges suggested by various technical folk. It didn't work every time and I never knew whether I would be able to use the windlass or not which made getting away from an anchorage with a heavy anchor and up to forty metres of chain a rather uncertain business.

Prickly Bay in Grenada is a very sociable pace, with a big population of cruising boats, most of which are owned by Americans who come down for the northern winter, sail up and down the islands then return to Prickly Bay, leaving their boats there in hurricane cradles and heading home for summer. Americans love to create a home from home when they are cruising and the daily VHF net reflected this with its endless talk of the women's domino group and baking classes. Some of the announcements bore little relation to anything nautical and were pretty toe-curling to listen to. I was beginning to realise that there were many cruising people, mostly ladies, who just love to talk on the radio. I often wondered why they didn't just stay at home and save themselves all the travel.

WHAT NEXT?

I was starting to wonder about the year ahead. I could stay in the Caribbean until about May but then I would either have to leave the boat secured on a special cradle for the hurricane season, which would be very expensive, or I could sail back towards the Azores and Europe, winding up back where I had started. But I was 64 and I felt that if I headed back all the acclimatisation I had gone through would be wasted. I doubted very much if I would have the energy to set off again and I had to admit to myself that as far as getting into the real cruising life the dream would probably be over. I was starting to relax and learning more each day about long-term life aboard. I no longer missed the world of work, my feet were getting brown, and even if I couldn't catch fish I was gradually making the transition from one lifestyle to the other and enjoying the process.

Over the past few months I had met some very experienced cruising folk, like John and Wendy, on the other *Beyond*, and I envied their outlook and general approach to life. I knew that I was far from being an old hand but I rather liked the idea of becoming one. About this time Helen, an old sailing friend and crew from racing days on the Clyde, who was now living in New Zealand, emailed to say that she hoped I would go down there to enjoy the Rugby Union World Cup and that if I could make it by the end of September, she could get me a ticket to see Scotland play England in Auckland. Worries about Panama came back again but Christine seemed to have enjoyed her trip down the Portuguese Coast enough to want to come back and had volunteered to come to the Canal Zone and then sail to the Galapagos Islands. I knew that if I turned back and sailed home I would probably regret it for the rest of my dull shore-bound days. I might even wind up going back to work.

I thought about it for a while but there really wasn't any choice. I would go through the canal and head off across the Pacific. In the back of my mind was the possibility that I would sell *Beyond* in New Zealand and fly home but I thought no further than that.

42

First I had to get to St Lucia to try and get my mechanical problems sorted out and, after a very sociable spell in Grenada, I headed north. A couple of mosquito bites on my ankle had become infected, swelling the joint badly. The infection was threatening to spread and I had to sort that out so I called at Carriacou, where the pharmacist sent me to see Doctor Freddy, a very friendly Cuban who was something of a local legend. His surgery was on the first floor of a tin roofed shack with lurid posters on the walls of the waiting area illustrating the dangers of alcoholism, unprotected sex and drug abuse. His patients clearly enjoyed life to the full. He prescribed some pills which by their size looked more suitable for use by a vet, but they did the trick and after a few days the infection began to reduce and I headed up to Bequia, and on to St Lucia.

The sailing between the islands was often tough going. I was usually hard on the wind and it would build strongly in the afternoons. I could see the bands of squally cloud coming through and the wind would get up to about twenty eight knots, ahead of the rain, which would pour down for about ten minutes with the boat flying along. When I saw one of these squalls coming I would roll away the genoa, ease the sheets and bear away sailing the boat like a dinghy, sitting up to weather with one hand on the mainsheet and the other on the wheel. Great fun.

Then as quickly as it had come, the rain would stop, the sky would clear and the wind would die, leaving me wallowing around in a sweaty calm for about 20 minutes after which things gradually got back to normal. The wind came back, building until l was hard on the wind again, going well until the next load of crap came through. I was usually pretty tired by the time I got the hook down in the evening.

Sailing towards Bequia I had been keeping my eyes on a squall which seemed to be heading in my direction. Sure enough it arrived at the same time as I did, sweeping down over the hill with the attendant torrential rain cutting visibility drastically. Without being able to run the engine with any certainty, I dumped the genoa and sailed under two reefed main.

I could handle the boat but the bay was new to me and I had a busy time trying to see where I was on the plotter which was below at the chart table. It was very challenging sailing the boat, trying to spot a mooring and getting a line ready for it, in amongst the other boats trying to stay out of trouble. Single-handed sailing is much like flying an aircraft - the middle bit is easy and most of the problems arise when you are either taking off or landing.

When I got to the beautiful island of St Lucia the Volvo guy looked over the engine and then took me on a guided tour of its essential organs, such as the heat exchanger and the starter motor, most of which it appeared were about to fail, or like two of the mountings, had already done so. Certainly, he said he would be able to source the bits for the pump in a week or so but, in his view, I would be throwing money away sales talk for sure. He asked if I had considered a new engine?

It was out of the question. I had already had to dip into my small savings account once or twice since leaving, when pension income had failed to match overdraft facility and there wasn't much left. The conversation continued in the cockpit with a beer and I began to see the sense of what he was saying but I had fallen into this trap once before after going into a car dealers to sort out a problem and coming out with a new car so I was wary to say the least.

But the arguments in favour were strong. I was headed for the Panama Canal, which connects the Atlantic Ocean to the Pacific Ocean and then across the huge expanse of the Pacific. If the engine quit at the canal, or worse still half way through, they would lash *Beyond* alongside a launch, take her through and give me a bill which would probably be not far short of what I was being asked to pay for a new engine. Not only that, they would impound the boat until I paid and to top it all I would, of course, still have to mend the engine.

Not for the first time since leaving home I went to bed worrying. In the months running up to my departure from the UK, I had thought much about the weather, sails, the rig, food and medical stuff but what few difficulties I had experienced had all arisen from technical stuff; the fridge, engine, alternator and steering bearings. The sailing was easy. It was the reality of my new life for sure but it didn't fit with my vision of becoming a bronzed ocean gypsy, rolling down the trades from one palm-fringed island to another, sailing the boat, catching fish and living the simple life.

Next day I looked at the costs and ran through the logic of it all. Quite apart from avoiding what could be a catastrophe in the canal and further problems down the line, the psychological benefit of removing all background uncertainties surrounding the present situation would be huge. Savings would take a big hit for sure but I consoled myself that numbers in a savings book weren't much use if I was stranded somewhere with a wrecked engine. Maybe I was taking the easy way out but I bit the bullet and signed up for a new engine.

6

Serendipity

Look for the Silver Lining

ALTHOUGH replacing the engine was clearly the right thing to do, the thought of the effect it would have on my already small store of savings did little to cheer me up. But every cloud has a silver lining and before long I began to look on my enforced stay in St Lucia in a new light.

Back in Prickly Bay I had noticed a white boat with the single word *Shipping* in large letters along the topsides. I guessed she was sponsored. I had passed her stern one morning on the way to the dinghy dock and, thinking no more of it, exchanged polite waves with two ladies in the cockpit. She was flying the Argentinean flag and looked to have come some distance.

Now in the Marina in Rodney Bay I saw her again and, having spent my entire working life in the shipping industry, my curiosity got the better of me and I walked over to say hello. I told them I was from Scotland to which they replied: "That's a long way."

They had come up from Argentina, via Brazil and Trinidad and were going on up to Martinique but they had just changed fuel filters and now they had problems with air in their system.

I offered to help and they looked doubtful but we went down below where, surrounded by filters, paper towel, pumps and a can of diesel, the lady skipper explained, in Spanish, what the problem seemed to be. I don't speak Spanish but having had an engine of the same Japanese brand that used to exhibit the same problems, I made a couple of suggestions which we tried, whilst the other Argentinian lady and her French gentleman friend stood aside. I should learn to keep my mouth shut.

"Try that", I said to them and the beast burst into life.

I smiled modestly. Scotland to the rescue.

The lady skipper, who, I was beginning to realise, was far from unattractive beneath the coating of diesel and sweat, beamed.

I was in heaven. Then the villain of the piece gave a couple of violent shudders, gasped for fuel and stopped.

Eric, the French gentleman, smiled condescendingly, having, as I later discovered, tried the same cure twice already. The bastard.

Oh well, it was worth a try. We commiserated jointly in a mixture of languages and agreed that perhaps we should have a beer later and I headed for the showers.

Beer led to dinner with the skipper, where even the fact that neither of us could speak more than a few words of the other's language, couldn't hide the fact that there was something occurring. Close to midnight back at her boat, I struggled to find the appropriate way to say goodnight but some things just take care of themselves and I was still there at breakfast time. It was clear that my failings as diesel mechanic had been forgotten but later in the day as we enjoyed a lunch ashore came the news that smart ass Eric had fixed the engine, so *Shipping* would be sailing for Martinique the following day to keep up their schedule. It looked as if our brief encounter would be over so I threw myself wholeheartedly into another night of cementing diplomatic relations between Scotland and Argentina then crept back to *Beyond* at dawn and moved round to the yard to start on the engine. *Beyond* was in the cradle at nine in the morning and by five the old engine was out and the new one was sitting on the bearers. It was quite a day's work. I walked back to the marina in the evening hoping that something else had happened to keep *Shipping* and her skipper there but the pontoon was empty. They had gone.

The days that followed were filled with periods of frantic activity, flying spanners and laughing locals, urging me to relax and assuring me that everything would be fine.

"Don't trouble your heart skip. She'll fit."

Meantime, the new propeller was stranded somewhere between Europe and St Lucia, island hopping its way through the international freight forwarding system towards its destination.

With the boat in such a mess, internally, I got a bed in a small hotel nearby and in the evenings retreated there waiting for some sign from my new friend that the brief time we had spent together had meant something.

Eventually a text arrived in Spanish, which I immediately forwarded to my nephew, who is fluent in the language. Being a student he was in the pub but said he would translate it as soon as he got home. The time difference worked in my favour and, just as I was turning in, the English translation arrived.

Do you ever find that when something really good happens you just don't know what to do? I read and re-read the message, walked round and round the room, sat on the bed, walked round the room again and with all thought of sleep gone, went to the bar to let it sink in. No-one had talked to me in those terms in years. All the background worries about engines, money and missing propellers faded into insignificance. I don't know if it's possible to fall asleep with a spring in your step but I think I did.

First thing in the morning I got a reply translated and sent off, then it was back to the real world of hose adaptors, splitter diodes and missing propellers.

By the end of the week, more texts had been exchanged via my friendly translator, and my nephew, Angus, was starting to see his uncle in a new light. Aurora would wait for me in Martinique. The missing prop arrived and we launched. The sea trial went well, the boat's performance under power had been transformed and Egbert's boys had done a great job. Suddenly the money didn't seem to matter just as much.

My son, Robert, and his fiancée, Susanna, arrived and we spent a week sailing around. It was great to see them again and to give them the chance to relax on the boat, but my mind was elsewhere.

A few days later I said goodbye to St Lucia and sailed north to Martinique. The week that followed was one of the happiest I can remember. During the day, we drifted back and forth between the chandlers, the supermarket and the internet café, did odd jobs on our boats and immersed ourselves in the pleasure of each other's company. In the evenings we gathered with a group of like-minded sailing friends, from Portugal, Spain, France and Colombia, sometimes on board one the boats, other times ashore, sharing food and good humour, conducting crazy conversations in a mixture of languages. We made do with laughter and another glass of wine when even goodwill and the occasional theatrical gesture could not bridge the linguistic gap. And in the background, always, laughter and music; mostly Samba and jazz guitar as we quickly discovered that we had common tastes.

At night, anchored off the marina or in the shallow sweep of St Anna Bay, the boisterous winds of the sun scorched day died and as the growing moon rose above us we slept like children after a day at the seaside. Then, much later, as the sky lightened we spent lazy mornings together as the breeze blew through the open port and the rising sun touched the boat, heralding another day.

It was a wonderful time and it's hard to believe that it all really happened, but it did and for a rather weathered and slightly cynical Scottish gent in his sixties, these were days of exquisite pleasure. Regardless of what the future might bring, the moment had been well and truly seized; two people with similar but separate agendas enjoying a brief moment of companionship and shared tenderness.

But we had different paths to follow, Aurora, already a well-known figure in Argentinian sailing circles, was heading north to start her own solo Atlantic crossing and I was heading west, to set off on the next stage of my own adventure. So one morning our two boats sailed together down the channel and out into the bay, where we parted company, hitchhiking on opposite sides of the road.

7

Martinique and Panama

Alone again . . .

I had decided to break the journey to Panama by calling at Curacao and set off in that direction. The wind was perfect, about fourteen knots apparent, just out on the quarter with hardly a cloud in the sky and no rain squalls. The boat rolled along making a steady seven and half knots and, after sunset, I took down the main and let her run on the poled out jib only ensuring easy work for the monitor and a quiet night for me.

But despite the smooth progress the good weather and the happy hour beer, I felt wretched as the excitement of setting off on the next stage of the adventure dulled by the realisation that, regardless of my hopes to see Aurora again, it was likely to be at least eight months or more before I did and I knew from bitter experience that a lot can change in that time when you are living on memories. That night was perfect for sailing with barely a cloud to be seen and great visibility.

The full moon rose behind me just after dark and lit the seascape from horizon to horizon.

The second night out the Caribbean returned to form with building clouds bringing a couple of high energy rain squalls that had the boat flying along as I tried to figure out the best angle to cut across the front of the clouds to let them get through as fast as possible. A few hours of calm followed and I motored in the moonlight with the new engine purring sweetly, pumping amps into the batteries as it pushed us along. The new breeze arrived in the early hours and I got her sailing again, right on course broad reaching in flat water. My conscience prevents me sleeping when motoring, even in the open ocean, but under sail with the monitor steering and the Sea Me and AIS on, I snoozed happily wakened by the timer every half hour. I find that if I can get another hour's sleep during the afternoon it's no problem to see the night out this way.

With slower progress in the light wind I decided to divert to Bonaire, rather than arrive in Curacao after dark and so sailed in on the afternoon of the fourth day from Martinique. Anchoring is not allowed so I picked up a mooring off the shore just south of the marina.

I was weary and couldn't take much pleasure in my surroundings. After years of sailing on my own I was starting to realise that I didn't have the same appetite for it any more. My time in Martinique had shown me how important it was to have someone to share things with. I had just spent a wonderful week in the company of someone I had become very fond of and here I was sailing away. Somehow it all seemed rather pointless.

I stayed in Bonaire for a day then enjoyed a very windy, hot sail across to Curacao closing the land in the late afternoon, dropping sail, then motoring in through the almost totally concealed entrance to Spanish Water, where I joined the other anchored boats in the wide shallow lagoon.

Perhaps I caught Curacao at a bad time but I couldn't find much good about it. The anchorage in Spanish water, which was windy and wet, is an hour from town by bus which occasionally adheres to the timetable but rarely appears if it's raining. The town its self was grubby and, because it depends on cruise ship passengers, expensive. Half the shops are duty free jewellers, clothes shops, all selling the same thing. One street further back from all the shops were the Caribbean equivalent of pound shops with customers to match. Lots of people dressed in outsize diamond earrings and massive gold chains, and that's just the men. The people in the bank seemed to have perfected the art of doing things at a snail's pace and the Immigration man took calls on his personal mobile while looking over the forms I had just filled in. I got the impression that visiting white people were tolerated because they brought in money. Oh well, maybe my bank was not so bad after all. I did manage to buy a new pair of cheap deck shoes and get a three month haircut, so I left looking a little like a convict but it only took one cup of water to wash it.

After a final couple of days spent trudging from Immigration to Customs and then the supermarket, while ferrying cans of fuel from the dock, I was ready to go. Water was, apparently unavailable, with the taps at the fish market by the dinghy dock padlocked. I was running low so on the last evening I took my jerry can along to a nearby diner where I ate some overpriced pasta. I paid the bill, tipped the waiter and asked if he would fill the can. Off he went and returned with ten litres. Five dollars US please. Thank you, and good night, Curacao.

Next morning I motored out and set off on the final Atlantic leg of my voyage, heading for Panama. I had been warned to stay well off the Venezuelan coast because of the acceleration effect on the wind and had heard lots about the very unpleasant seas that often ran at the corner, which someone in Martinique had described as the Cape Horn of the Caribbean. So once past the western tip of Curacao, I headed well up to the northwest.

For the first couple of days it did blow hard and there was a steep and unpleasant sea, particularly along the area north of Aruba. The weather was on the quarter, rough and windy but not really malicious. Every so often an out-of-sequence sea would rear up and over take us at a different angle from the rest, throwing the stern around and giving the monitor a hard time. To add to it, the moon that had lit my way from Martinique was as good as done and for the first few days the night sailing began to take on a rather menacing aspect. But we were making great progress and on one day I managed 167 miles in 24 hours with just the poled out jib and the monitor steering.

Every morning I would run the engine for an hour to top up the batteries and clutched it in to give it some work to do. On the third morning it started as usual but when I engaged forward there was the violent vibration. I tried neutral, which was fine, then astern, which was even worse.

I immediately thought there must be a rope around the prop and checked around the decks but there was no sign of a stray end and, anyway, if there had been it would probably have stalled the engine. I stopped it, made a cup of coffee and had a think. Bent blade? Unlikely. Had the fairing pad above the sail drive fallen down onto the prop? It was possible but also unlikely. How ironic to have paid all that money for a new engine so that I could have a trouble-free passage through the canal and across the Pacific only to have this happen.

We were still sailing fast and it was far too rough to stop the boat and go over the side for a look so I rolled away the jib, sailed the boat in a circle, then headed up into the wind and let her drop back and start making sternway, bringing her stern round, then bearing away again hoping that whatever might be round the prop would drop clear.

Back on course I re-started the engine and tried again, but no luck, same thing. Oh Shit. One of the drawbacks of being on your own is that there is no-one to share the problems with so you don't get any outside view. However, thanks to the wonder of satellite email, I was able to contact my engineering mate in St. Lucia and explained the problem. He agreed that it was most likely something round the prop but suggested checking the mountings with the engine in neutral, which I did, then put a spanner on them to be doubly sure. They were fine. I also checked the seal around the sail drive exit, also fine. Oh well, at least there was a good breeze. Keep calm and carry on under sail.

Thankfully, although the breeze did ease down, it held sufficiently to keep me moving and on the morning of March 7 after a busy 24 hours dodging the shipping converging on the canal, I sailed in through the breakwaters of Cristobal, attracting the wrath of Port

Control and one of the pilot boats. I got the main down and the anchor ready and put out as many fenders as I had on each side. I had emailed ahead to the marina at Shelter Bay explaining that I might need some assistance to get alongside, but despite being right on my ETA and calling them repeatedly on the VHF, there was no response. At noon I sailed in to the marina entrance with a half rolled headsail out. There was no-one there but I spotted a gap at the end of one of the pontoons and sailed into it, rolling away the headsail at the last moment, and lassoing one of the cleats to bring her to a halt.

It was stinking hot and I was soaked in sweat but I secured the boat as if I did this sort of thing every day and sat down with some great relief. I was mighty weary.

It was also not the triumphant, diesel-fuelled, perfectly controlled engine purring arrival I had planned but I was there; Panama, gateway to the Pacific. Later in the afternoon I got the snorkel on and went under the boat, where to my great relief I found a tangle of polypropylene fishing rope, bits of net and polypropylene twine, tangled and floating around the prop.

I cut it away, the prop was fine and the engine ran smoothly both ahead and astern. To make the day complete, Christine arrived on board from home.

SHELTER BAY
Strange Days Indeed . . .

Before it became a marina, Shelter Bay was a US base where troops were trained in jungle warfare before being shipped off to whichever country the Good 'Ole USA happened to be liberating at the time. Local business interests now run the marina. The old administration buildings have been converted into offices, a bar and a restaurant and there's a lot of fresh paint around but the jungle still comes right down to the compound.

Yachts transiting the canal used to wait at the Yacht Club over at the flats. But the premises became the subject of a demolition order instigated, some say, by the same business interests who were developing the marina. The story goes that despite efforts to save the club the bulldozers moved in during the early hours of the morning on the appointed date and in a few minutes' generations of cruising tradition were ground into the dirt. That's progress, I guess.

The marina was something of an enigma; it should have been a pleasure to stay there. It certainly cost enough, but somehow the whole place just succeeded in annoying its cruising clients. The charging scale started at 40 feet, seemingly smaller boats did not exist and whilst I was there a couple of very large and immaculate motor yachts owned by named celebrities arrived and stayed for a few days.

As a visiting yachtie, if you needed assistance of any sort you waited outside the office and took a ticket with your turn number on it. It could take anything up to half an hour to actually get inside, and even then it was quite usual to be completely ignored for five or ten minutes whilst the marina folk chatted amongst themselves in Spanish, tucked into snacks or talked on their mobiles. It's the only place I can recall where I have had to wait in a queue to give someone the opportunity to be rude to me. Yet on some days everyone could be so helpful and it was very odd indeed.

The Immigration and Customs people made occasional and seemingly unscheduled appearances at their tiny, anonymous office round the back of the marina building. When I presented my papers for inward clearance the first thing the official did was demand $20 "overtime." I wanted to point out that it was a Wednesday afternoon but diplomacy prevented me.

Regardless of the official cost of the clearance itself you clearly had to pay to play.

This sort of thing happened over and over again during our stay. The rules, such as they were, seemed to keep changing and even then they were not applied consistently, with one boat being told one thing, and the next one would get a completely different story later the same day. I had hired an agent and it was well worth it. He was excellent and, apart from inward clearance the inspection and the mandatory fumigation, he took care of everything. He also managed to put some pressure on the overtime brigade to produce my cruising permit, one of the several vital pieces of paper required before I could transit. Before he intervened I had been told that I would have to go up to Panama City and pay an addition $50 for the bit of paper the onsite official said he needed to authorise him to issue the actual permit on site. It was simply nuts. My agent had a chat with him and the document was duly produced, straight away, for twenty dollars. I admired the people who were doing this on their own. I would not have had the patience.

Against this background the transit dates for some yachts kept being changed. An eight to ten day wait seemed about usual but we were told that if we cared to produce $2000 in cash we would transit immediately. I am pretty sure some of the bigger boats on tightly scheduled delivery, to whom $2000 was a flea bite, did this and that was what caused the slippage amongst the cruising poor.

At about five each evening, a crowd of us would gather in the bar to swap rumours and commiserate with each other. The staff in the bar had perfected the art of ignoring their customers but we persevered and the evening "management meetings "as they became known were very social affairs.

John Woolfe, from the other *Beyond*, had been less fortunate in his choice of agent and summed it up for all of us when he sat down wearily one evening and asked for a cold beer and a jar of Vaseline. "I am meeting my agent at six," he added. "I know I am going to get screwed."

As darkness fell, the surrounding jungle would come alive with a background chorus of screeches, squawks and croaks, against which the packs of howler monkeys gave voice. The first time I heard them I thought it was a football crowd in some nearby stadium, but, no, it was the howlers living up to their name. They are very territorial and give voice whenever anyone looks like moving into the neighbourhood.

The whole atmosphere of the voyage changed at Panama. In the Caribbean, *Beyond* had been one of hundreds of boats that had crossed the Atlantic and one amongst many more that were long-term Caribbean residents and rarely moved away from the islands. The annual arrival of the rally fleets in the area brings an almost obscene display of European yachting opulence, where every boat you see seems to have every conceivable shiny accessory bolted to its stern or lashed to its coach roof. The children of the owners sit in the quayside cafes playing with their laptops or run around the pontoons on shiny scooters, their designer sunglasses saving them from the glare of polished topsides and stainless steel. I admire the business acumen of anyone who can figure out a way to get people to pay to sail across the Atlantic Ocean, but I am not a rally person. For me the joy of crossing an ocean is in being out on your own, away from the crowd, independent and free to roam. I felt a bit uncomfortable with the culture that sees over two hundred boats arrive in St Lucia every year proudly flying their rally flags. I often wondered how they thought the rest of us got there but I doubt if they cared and it didn't matter anyway.

In Panama the people are different and so are many of the boats. There is very little opulence here because many of the boats waiting to transit had started their voyages back in New Zealand, Australia or South Africa years previously and were now on their way home. Those of us who had recently started had made the commitment to leave the Atlantic and pass through the great doorway to the Pacific, with its massive distances, scattered islands and intriguing atmosphere of romance.

Compared with the irritations of staying in Shelter Bay, our canal transit was a pleasure. Our tyres and lines arrived the day before transit and on the appointed day with John and Wendy from *Beyond* as line handlers, along with Chris, a new friend from the States, we set off to anchor in the flats to await the pilot. There was a strong wind blowing directly onto the pontoon and getting away was rather tricky especially as the boat, which normally steers very precisely in astern, seemed to have taken a mind of its own. But we got clear and motored over to the anchorage. There was certainly a strange feel to the boat. She seemed to be over correcting but with such a strong wind on the quarter, and knowing I tend to always fear the worst, I kept my concerns to myself.

Yachts under fifty feet in length don't take a pilot but use an advisor instead. These guys are canal employees, tug or workboat captains, who are good boat handlers and have a fantastic knowledge of the parts of the canal that big transiting ships never see. The first advisor, friendly, helpful and relaxed, boarded around five and we motored into the locks at Gatun, lashed alongside a stunning all carbon boat big enough to require a pilot. Alongside such a powerful yacht we had little to do as far as the engine was concerned but we took responsibility for the starboard quarter line, which John and Wendy handled really well. Chris and Christine took the bow. With the stern lines led through the cleat and onto the primary winch, taking up the slack was easy, and with occasional guidance from our advisor, we managed to cope well with the inrush of water. It surged to the surface from the culverts in the lock floor, quickly raising the level in the lock so that we could motor into the next chamber. We emerged into the Gatun Lake just as it was getting dark and secured to the swinging buoy and our advisor leaving us to head home for the evening.

Gatun Lake was created by damming the Chagres River and flooding the valley. The lake is fresh water, although a strange colour, and is home to much jungle related wildlife including crocodiles. We were feeling mighty pleased with ourselves and, after a really good feed, we sat in the cockpit with the lantern hung on the backstay and toasted our success. The howlers made a lot of noise in the jungle ashore, the moon came up and the rum went down. Before long we were all in fine form, and as midnight approached and common sense receded, Chris, our American friend, jumped in and we followed; swimming round the boat in the moonlight, cracking crocodile jokes and laughing at our own stupidity. I wonder what the howlers thought of it all? A month later in the Galapagos I met the folk from Duetto, homeward bound to NZ after a long circumnavigation, who told me that they had actually seen a couple of crocodiles in daylight just close to the buoy.

We must be being preserved for a very special fate.

The next morning the second advisor arrived early and we set off across the lake and on through the canal. We had heard many stories about how difficult advisors and pilots could be but ours could not have been better and put us completely at our ease. They were also a great source of knowledge and it was a pleasure to have them aboard during the trip. I was struck by the fact that in all my travels so far, this was the first place where I had heard locals speak highly of their government.

Getting through Panama was a significant step for me and marked the transition from what had started as an almost temporary venture into Atlantic cruising, to a commitment to the kind of life I had been reading about for so many years. In the Atlantic I could easily have turned round and sailed back to Europe, or laid the boat up in the Caribbean for the hurricane season, gone home and come back the next year. I knew that once I had gone through the canal and set off across the ocean that lay ahead there was no way back. Like a learner jumping out of a plane with a parachute for the first time, I had some misgivings. I hoped, of course, that I would end up in New Zealand but what a huge mass of sea lay between *Beyond* and that far country.

I knew the season was right for a departure from Panama and my aim was to end up in New Zealand by the end of September but I had given very little thought to the timings of the various legs of the trip or even to which islands I would call at. It was hugely exciting. I would have to get to the Galapagos first, then take on the long voyage from the Galapagos to the Marquesas, about 3000 miles of open ocean away. It was a longer solo voyage than I had ever done before but it would all be downwind. After that the distances looked much less daunting and there were so many islands to choose from.

I was a bit concerned about the steering but as we motored round to the anchorage I felt that I was about to step out into a whole new world.

8

The Galapagos

"It is not the strongest who survive, or the most intelligent who survive, it is those who can adapt"

Darwin

AFTER two weeks in the Canal Zone I certainly didn't want to hang around any longer, despite my slight misgivings about the way the boat was steering. Christine was booked on a flight from the Galapagos which we were going to struggle to catch. We talked it over the night we got through and anchored in Balboa. The weather on passage was likely to be light. I had a good boat and a good friend to sail with. There didn't seem much more to say about it and the next day we set of for the Enchanted Islands, eight days to the west.

After a short spell of motoring the breeze set in and, for the rest of the trip, we had mainly moderate and occasionally light weather but we made good progress under the scorching sun. It was so hot it was impossible to stand on the wooden deck in bare feet and one day we left a metal pan out in the sun to see if it would get hot enough to fry an egg. We didn't quite manage it but it was certainly too hot to touch. We frequently passed big logs, some the size of telegraph poles, but thankfully managed to avoid them although their presence was a concern during the night hours. One day we sailed through a huge area of very disturbed water, interspersed with massive areas of glassy smoothness, even though the wind was still blowing steadily across the surface of the water. It was very strange and I wondered if this was caused by some sort of upwelling of water of a different temperature.

In the Canal Zone many people had told us how good the fishing was in the Pacific so I had another go and we trailed the line for a few days. The only action occurred whilst I was sleeping and, according to Christine, a huge marlin took the lure, leapt out of the water and took off with the whole rig; just as well the line parted. That was enough for me. On another occasion a single white light appeared on the horizon astern at twilight and for hours and hours it seemed to be following us, gradually getting closer. We had heard about a number of yachts which had got into problems with opportunist pirates off the Venezuelan coast and were slightly worried about it. Just before midnight we put our navigation and cabin lights off and sailed along in complete darkness. Thankfully, by morning the other boat, whatever it had been, had gone.

The wind and swell were nearly always on the quarter, and the monitor steered all the way but I could see that it was struggling at times, and seemed to be over correcting. I spent a while watching the linkage from the wheel moving the stock. With the emergency tiller socket showing when the stock was fore and aft, it seemed that the rudder was amidships when the stock was about ten degrees over to port. By compensating with the steering lines I managed to fool the monitor into thinking the helm was neutral and I tuned out most of the difference on the auto pilot with the helm alignment adjustment so that it would steer after a fashion in the calm patches. As long as the swell remained at a constant angle to the stern it did remarkably well. There was nothing else I could do, there was no way back, and with our destination downwind, continuing was the only option. Apart from the nagging worry about the steering, the trip was a real pleasure. We were two handed and worked two on two off, making good progress under a big moon and glorious, almost cloudless, days, eating and sleeping well, crossing the equator heading South, on the same day as the sun crossed it heading north for the summer. This was Christine's first long sea passage and she took to it well, submitting herself to a short but essential Crossing the Line ceremony as part of which she received a soaking in cold sea water, a large rum and a certificate signed by Father Neptune. It was a wonderful trip and on more than one night our course was such that we sailed right down the path of moonlight on the water. It was beautiful. We crossed the Meridian of 90 degrees west late on the last night out. *Beyond* had sailed one quarter of the way around the world.

We sailed into Academy Bay on the morning of March 26 with rays swimming around the boat and sea lions popping their heads up to watch us go by. The recent tsunami had caused a lot of damage along the shore and the sea had inundated the Immigration office which had been relocated, but no-one seemed to know where it now was. We spent hours driving around the countryside in taxis before we finally located it. In the evening, with everything organised, we relaxed and celebrated our safe arrival with a great meal ashore. The next day my ever-cheerful and resourceful shipmate headed off to catch the first of a series of flights back to Scotland and I got on with trying to figure out just what was wrong with the boat. I knew we had been very lucky with the weather, but the next leg of the trip was a three week solo passage to the Marquesas Islands and I had to find out just what was going on and fix it because I certainly wasn't setting off the way things were.

So the next morning I clamped the wheel amidships, put in the emergency tiller, lashing it amidships as well, so that there was no way the stock could rotate. Then I got into the water with the weights on and ducked down to the rudder, grabbed the trailing edge of the rudder blade and swung on it. My worst fears were confirmed, I could move the blade from side to side through about twenty degrees. No wonder the boat had been sailing like a drunk all the way from Panama.

I got back on board, made some coffee, and had a think. As far as I could see there were two possibilities, either the welds had failed between the tangs and the stock internally, which seemed the most likely explanation, or the tangs were moving from side to side inside the blade. I certainly couldn't carry on without doing some sort of repair and, as far as I knew, there was no way of getting the boat out of the water. I would have to float the rudder out and get it ashore so that I could have a good look at it.

As a precaution, I laid out a second anchor with the dinghy and hove the warp as tight as I could. The bay is pretty much wide open to the Pacific and there is always a swell. But, thankfully, there was very little wind and the weather looked settled. I called a surveyor friend back home in Scotland and we talked over the problem and likely solutions. I sometimes feel modern communications are a mixed blessing but they kept coming to my aid. Jim agreed to speak to the designer and find out what the internal arrangement was and get back to me.

First thing next morning the agent put me in touch with a repair firm who clearly understood the problem. They responded immediately, arriving on board within a few hours, complete with dive gear and large box of spanners and by late afternoon they had the rudder out, and in their rib. A quick check showed that not only was the stock rotating independently of the blade, it was also moving from side to side on its vertical axis. We ran the rib ashore and transferred the rudder to a trailer for transport to the workshop. That was about all we could do for one day and I went back aboard to sit and worry my way through a sleepless night. The weather was still settled and I had two anchors down but no rudder. The only conclusion I could come to was that whatever we did we should do it as quickly as possible even if we wound up with a fairly rough and ready solution. As long as it locked the blade relative to the stock that would do to get me to somewhere where I could get a permanent repair and that probably meant Tahiti. It was a long way. I spent a lot of time drinking tea and sketching out possible solutions but until we could open up the blade and see exactly what was wrong, I could only guess.

Nights filled with worry are long nights and the morning seemed to take very long black hours to come but it did come eventually. Just after seven Jaime, who owned the repair company, picked me up at the quay in the jeep and we headed out of town the workshop where they had already opened up the blade. Those guys didn't hang around.

What a mess. There had originally been three tangs, two horizontal and one at forty five degrees to the bottom of the stock. The welds had failed on the top two, long ago long ago by the look of them. This put all the stress on the bottom one which had finally given up and fractured about an inch out from the stock; probably during the rough following seas between Curacao and Panama. It looked as if had only been the buoyancy of the blade which had stopped it dropping off altogether. Thank goodness we had had light to moderate weather from Balboa to the Islands. I began to realise just how lucky I was to have got to Galapagos at all. I could well have been out there still steering with some sort of jury rudder. Someone must, indeed, have been watching over me.

It didn't take long to settle on a method of repairing the steel damage and we welded up a stronger stainless framework based on the original design. Not having the correct high density foam, but needing a fast solution, we bedded the framework in and then epoxied over it. The temperature was in the nineties and the boys had to work fast. There was a lot of good natured crack going on in Spanish and, with the workshop radio blaring out some local music, the grinders flew, foam was applied and the glass cloth was cut. No risk assessment, method statement or health and safety manual, just a bunch of good natured guys who knew exactly what to do and seemed to really enjoy getting on with it.

It was a long day, with only a brief pause for lunch and a few occasional stops for water but by evening we were well ahead and, as I walked down the dusty lava road from the workshop to the main road to grab a lift back to the dock, I began to realise just how far I had come. In the gloom of the small hours it had seemed that the best I could hope for was some sort of quick and ugly fix. Now what we had was, undoubtedly, very strong and I hoped permanent because we could probably never get it apart again.

By mid-morning the following day, the rudder arrived at the dock faired freshly anti-fouled and looking good as new. We ferried it out in the rib and got it up into the trunking only to find that in our eagerness to reinforce the stock housing we had built it up too much. The top of the blade was hitting the bottom rudder tube bearing before the stock was fully home. We took it back out and into the rib and re-shaped it with a grinding tool and a rasp. There was plenty of material to work with, and after a bit more fine adjustment, we had the whole thing back in place. The quadrant was secured on the key and the steering linkage re connected.

The wheel turned smoothly from hard over to hard over. The rudder moved as it was designed to and sat perfectly amidships with the Turk's Head on the wheel at twelve o'clock which was something it hadn't done for a while. No more would the monitor spin the wheel from side to side trying to get the boat to respond. The auto pilot should now be able to steer in a calm, since the rudder blade would be where the feedback arm said it was, not at some indeterminate angle., one way or the other. Even the allegedly Smart Pilot with gyro sensing couldn't have been expected to cope with that.

I was back in business, the initial gloom and worry of the past days replaced by a feeling of tremendous relief and gratitude to these good people who had worked so fast and so hard and cheerfully to help me. We sat in the cockpit and I thanked them as sincerely as I could. My Spanish may have been imperfect but they knew what I meant.

Repairing the rudder internals, Galapagos

With the rudder repaired I could finally take a more relaxed look at my new surroundings. Yachts calling at the Galapagos are required to appoint an agent, whether they want one or not because the Port Captain, who is a career Naval Officer and a VIP doesn't want to be dealing with a bunch of tatty yachties all day. Well, would you? The regulations governing visiting yachts seem to be designed to stop external operators bringing in charter guests and to ensure that all island visiting is done in the local cruise boats, of which there are many, and in fairness most looked very well run.

There are only two ports of entry in the group and a visiting yacht may stay for up to 20 days in the port of arrival but if you want to cruise to any other island you must have a cruising permit. To get one of these you start applying to the Ecuadorian Government, in Spanish, about a year before you want to visit because it can take that long. Even if, and when, you are lucky enough to be granted a cruising permit, you have to pay $100 per person on board for each day you are in the area and you must carry, pay, accommodate and feed a local guide whilst you are cruising the islands. Not surprisingly, most yachts enter at Academy Bay, or Wreck Bay, then stay there doing their exploring on the charter boats.

The degree to which the various regulations are applied seems to depend on the way in which the current Captain of Port interprets them and no-one actually warned me not to visit any other island but I am sure the Navy would take great delight in fining anyone who transgressed. But the islands have to preserve their fabulous natural heritage and their tourism industry so who can blame them for doing their best to protect their fragile market?

I liked the place very much, for its cleanliness, its laid back and unsophisticated atmosphere and the smiling and helpful attitude of everyone I met. No in-your-face, aggressive cruise ship driven Barbados-style economy here. Puerto Ayora thrives on its own resources, most of them natural. As in a lot of remote islands, the people have a no-nonsense approach and, as I found with the rudder repair, they just get on with it. There are a lot of small businesses where they still actually mend things. I called at a mechanics for some fuel filters and at the back they were mending marine engines, motor cycles and a selection of domestic stuff. There was a workshop where they would cut and shape steel for you and where they still sold individual nuts and bolts, studding iron and strong, well-made tools.

Down along the main road closer to the harbour there were dive shops and bars and a fish market on the shore where the catch was landed daily, to be sold immediately to the crowd of waiting customers. Pelicans strutted around and gruff voiced sea lions flopped about around the market, feeding on scraps, almost too fat to move. Every now and again the stallholder would take a swipe at one of them with a broom but it was all just part of a game. One morning traffic was brought to a halt by three pelicans arguing over bits of a tuna in the middle of the road. No-one seemed to mind and it all added of the charm of this lovely place.

A little further out of the centre, there were galleries and some fairly expensive jewellers, turning out what appeared to my uneducated eye to be very high quality stuff, mostly of silver. I had been meaning to get some form of personal identification for some time, in case I was ever washed up on a beach somewhere, or became so wandered I couldn't remember who I was. So I went to one of the shops and had them make me an identity tag with my name on one side and my passport number on the other. The person I spoke to was a delightful Swiss lady and she took a real interest in the idea and made a beautiful job of it, signing it in one corner. It's round my neck as I write and I sincerely hope it stays there for a long time to come.

The atmosphere in the evenings was laid back and friendly with the various internet cafes full of Lonely Planet type people and the bars selling really good food at very reasonable prices. There was none of the hustle and blast of the Caribbean or the intimidating feeling we had got in Panama here, just a lot of very relaxed, smiling friendly people whom it was a pleasure to be around.

Down at the harbour amongst some trees there were two volleyball courts and almost every evening there would be a match on under the lights, watched by a small crowd, with kids running around on skateboards and generally enjoying themselves. The area seemed to be the focal point at which people gathered of an evening to chat or stroll around.

Out in the Bay under the stars the water taxis plied back and forward from the shore and the yachts rolled quietly in the swell. I began to hear rumours from other sailors about the very high price of food in Polynesia and I did my best to stock up with as much as I could before I left and laid in the requisite number of bottles of beer to cover the trip. By now I had adopted a very simple formula, two small bottles for each day of the passage, plus four extra for safe arrival celebrations. It would have been inviting bad luck not to give thanks for the completion of the voyage and on *Beyond* I never considered the voyage over until safe arrival drinks were served. I never carried wine or spirits on the boat. If the trip looked like lasting longer than planned I would reduce to one sunset beer a day and if my stocks ran out, so be it, I would go without.

The morning I left I went ashore early to get some fresh bread. There was a modern white church across the road from the landing pier. Its doors were open and inside rows of uniformed school children stood and sang, the music spilling out onto the street.

Somehow that seemed to sum the whole place up for me.

9

Pacific Letters

It's a Long Way to Hiva Oa . . .

I left Academy Bay on a Friday, which by seafaring tradition you are not supposed to do, but I felt I had been there long enough. There had been no wind for days and there was none forecast until the following week. But the prospect of spending another four days rolling around in the swell didn't appeal and I always feel you are better to get on your way and see what happens. So I motored out and headed west. I had an idea that I might spend the night at Isabella Island but the land was shrouded in cloud and when I drew near the rain moved out to meet me, bringing a stiff breeze with it. I managed to sail for an hour or so, enjoying a good wash in the rain, before it died out. By that time it was too late to get in before dark so I motored again until I was ten miles off the land, stopped and secured the boat for the night, letting her drift slowly south.

By five the following morning I had had enough of the rolling and clattering. I got up and started the engine, heading off at economic revs but which way to head to find the wind? There was more chance of a breeze further south but I would be throwing away distance and I had only limited fuel. So I headed more or less southwest and motored off into the dawn.

Mid-morning I got a breeze that lasted about an hour but that was it and by noon I had covered just 80 miles since leaving the previous day. Mind you, under the circumstances that wasn't too bad, but it had cost precious fuel. Early afternoon brought more breeze and I managed to get her going along not too badly and we sailed for the rest of the day and into our second night.

At dawn on the third day the breeze died completely and I began to wonder whether I had been right to leave. At least I was about 200 miles down the long road to the Marquesas whilst the other boats were presumably still in Academy Bay. Anyway, the die was cast, and I certainly couldn't go back.

The question was: How long to keep motoring? When do you use your fuel? Now? Maybe not. Could be better to wait a day or so for the forecast breeze? But my mind was made up for me. Early in the afternoon the breeze came in again and we were off, sailing well with the wind on the quarter and making a steady six and a half knots, wake streaming out astern. The monitor was steering and I was quietly pleased with myself for not still being in Academy Bay watching the pelicans.

The next couple of days were busy with sail changes and rain squalls. We were still on the edge of the Doldrums but as the day drew to a close, things began to settle down a bit. What follows was written as the days went by.

Wednesday 13

Six hours' sleep and a grey morning with cloud all around. The boat was nodding along on her course at just over five knots with just the headsail on and I wondered how long she had been going that slowly but you can't be sleeping and trimming the sails at the same time. At this stage my priority has to be looking after the boat and myself and, if that means losing a few miles overnight, then so be it. I am after all cruising, there's no rush and there's a very long way to go.

So I sat in the hatch and had a cup of tea and watched the sun come up. If the weather is going to change it nearly always does it just after sun up or just before sun down, and usually the wind will shift a little and freshen as the morning goes on, building to a peak at about three in the afternoon and then ease back as the evening comes on. The clouds change at these times, too. The sun sucks the vapour off the sea during the day and in the early evening darker clouds, with a bit more vertical extent gather, bringing the chance of the odd squall during the night as the air cools and drops back to sea level.

So I shorten sail just before dark and let her take it easy through the night.

But this morning it's looking good - the sky clears, up comes the sun and in comes the breeze, another cup of tea, just to be sure, then up with the main again and we are off at six and half. Occasionally it is seven, which we maintain all morning, hitting 143 miles for the day at noon.

I dial in a new waypoint a few 100 miles down the track and we are off again keeping the speed up through the afternoon in the fresh breeze.

I always try and use intermediate waypoints because on a long passage, on a rumb line, if you use your destination as a waypoint you can be away off the track before the bearing to waypoint will change. So I set a series of stepping stones, usually a few hundred miles apart, and head for the next one down the course line; that way you stay close to the rumb line. The stepping stones approach gives you a psychological target that seems achievable because it's only a couple of hundred miles away instead of a couple of thousand. As the boat approaches each waypoint, I usually leapfrog it and start heading for the next one again and I always feel as if I am making progress.

It's the same nibbling approach that enables Pygmies to eat elephants.

Thursday 14

Wind held all night and we kept on with No4 and 2 reefs. Making good speed so should be a high mileage day. Very rough and confused as well around 0800/0900 but still making good speed. Will watch it and maybe go to jib alone if it keeps up. One hour's tea and contemplation in the rising sun.

Polished the coach roof port side right to it's for'd end, replaced the end strop on the whisker pole which was getting frayed by the uphaul clip. There's a bit of plastic hose on the new one so that won't happen again for a while at least.

164 miles at noon. 6.8 average, a boat best since leaving Panama. Hot, blue seas and sky and quite windy. Asparagus and boiled potatoes for lunch, followed by guitar practice.

It's a long way to Hiva Oa,
It's a long way by sea,

It's a long way to Hiva Oa, but that's where I long to be,
Goodbye Galapagos, farewell Academy Bay!
It's a long way to Hiva Oa,
But I'll get there some day.

Friday 15

Grey and overcast to start with and an awkward swell pushing the stern around making the monitor work too hard so I took down the main and let her go with the No4, still managing to make about six, but will have some tea and watch developments, maybe change up to the genoa after breakfast.

Think six knots is a good target speed and should be achievable with little or no strain on the boat.

Dull and rough. Not good for boat work, maybe revise the schedule today.

Noon. 167 miles, a record for the trip. Well done *Beyond*.

Sky clearing just after noon so set No 1 genoa; pulling well and doing just above target. From now its six knots, or better, if that can be achieved without stress on any part of the boat.

If boat stressed, or I feel she is struggling, then I will reduce until it all settles down.

We are in the favourable Equatorial current right now, and next week we may have an adverse current but we will worry about that when it happens, not that there is anything I can do about it anyway. So time for lunch.

Oops! My collection of Galapagos potatoes has gone off and I was really looking forward to them. I managed to save about a dozen but the rest were soft and some had gone black and mushy, that was after only a week.

Clearly these were not Darwinian survivors. They could not adapt.

Saturday 16

A grey start with heavy rain at 0600 so up in the cockpit for a good shower. I am now truly fresh. Wind dropped in the rain and veered, so we were heading about 280 for a while, then it did the usual thing and worked its way back round to SE and picked up again. Two boiled eggs for breakfast, bread all mouldy so threw it out yesterday. Tortillas now and when I see how the gas is lasting I will bake a couple of baguettes.

End of first week, celebration meal last night, sausage casserole (freeze-dried) with extra potatoes and chocolate pudding. A great evening, just a pity there was no one to share it with.

Wind all over the place in the evening, lots of sail changes, main up then down, poled out No 1 as well as genoa, then No 1 down as wind freshened, then big clouds gathering and heavy rain at dusk, secured pole, wash boards in.

Up till 0100, wind veered and dropped in the rain, then freshened again. Genoa on green, then out, then greens for the night.

Sunday 17

Rain eased and stopped about 0100. Genoa out. Off to bed.

0630 sky cleared, sun coming up, could be a dry day, steady progress at about five and a half through the night. Cups of tea and the Eagles, good Sunday morning stuff. Reminds me of home.

I will wait for an hour or so to see what the wind does when the sun is up properly.

Just after nine set the No 1 on the pole and had great sailing all morning in lovely weather, steady breeze out on the quarter.

137 at noon, 5.7, so doing OK! Great sailing all afternoon with the two headsails out.

Evening: Bit of an increase in the wind so took the No 1 in at about half ten and left the pole up.

Beautiful moonlit night, no cloud, boat siding along, light as day. Fantastic. Moon dreaming in the cockpit. Tea and biscuits then off to bed at about 2330. I am easily pleased.

Monday 18

Nice morning, been sailing high all night by the look of things, around 210/ 220. But speed seems to have been quite good, high fives? Tea in the sun then set the No 1 again at about 0800. Sausages and fried bread for breakfast, plus some pears and coffee. Milk had gone off, swapped over to Carnation. Ok in tea and coffee.

Good sailing all morning, boat work etc. Carried on with the coach roof side polishing but lost the jug of very expensive Panama polish over the side. I couldn't believe it. I had carefully laid it on top of the coach roof, and while I was rubbing, I heard a thump and just assumed that it had fallen onto the side deck beside me. When I went to get more polish no sign of it. How could it have slid off the coach roof, onto the side deck then over the toe rail and over the side, without as much as a splash? But it must have done. I was unhappy. It had cost a lot but as well I was actually enjoying the progress I was making with the task and now that was it stuffed. Not a very happy morning. That container of polish was the nucleus of my boat work programme and I had torn up an old T-shirt to apply it and polish with. Now I will have to find something else to focus on, and another use for the rags.

Noon saw us clocking up 141 for the day, but that was with the half hour extra, so about 5.7 kts for the day. Not bad.

Likely ETA at that speed is Saturday 30, 12 days away that would be fine. Good sailing all afternoon with twin headsails. Wind easing towards the evening but still getting along. Some monitor adjustments, and sailing a little high, but steady progress nonetheless.

I will see what the evening brings and maybe leave the headsail up tonight?

Checked email but nothing from Aurora. I keep referring to her last which was very positive.

Egg fried rice for tea and a tin of pineapple. Very healthy stuff.

Wind went light about eleven and she was rolling with the headsails alternately flapping then filling, so took down the No1 and headed up a bit to fill the genoa, sailing slowly in the lighter wind at about four/five knots, and thirty degrees high of the course but at least the headsail is filing with a fairly taut sheet.

High cirrus and a halo round the moon. Wind tomorrow?

Tuesday 19

Slept through to five thirty, sailing about twenty degrees high but just on five knots so not too bad.

Boiled eggs and cornflakes for breakfast, set the No 1 again on the pole and going well by nine.

Fine sunny morning, going to be hot. Changed the knots on the monitor lines to see if that will stop them slackening off.

I am still mourning the loss of my polish. The edge has definitely gone off the maintenance programme.

Made a fiddle for the galley work top to stop everything sliding into the sink when she rolls. The concept was good with one piece of hardwood screwed to the worktop, and the other epoxied on top, hiding the screws but the top bit started to lift when the epoxy started curing. I had to screw it down then used the wrong drill size so wound up with two ugly screws and an extra hole. It's a good job I am not a cosmetic surgeon.

But it works. Nothing slides into the sink anymore.

Good sailing all morning in perfect weather, blue sky, blue sea.

Poor speed at noon, 125 miles only, due to the quiet overnight conditions.

I have given up on the idea of a target speed. I will set the sails to keep her comfortable and pointing more or less in the right direction and the speed can turn out to be whatever it turns out to be. From now on the criteria is stressless ambling. It's the way to go.

A snooze in the afternoon, then more Spanish. I hope I get the chance to use it. Nothing from Aurora again.??

The usual two beers at happy hour, plus nuts.

Omelette and fried potatoes for tea, plus pears and coffee.

Handed the No 1 at 2045 with the moon just rising. As the breeze seemed to be increasing, there was quite a bit of cloud around and she was dashing along a bit. The new speed policy in practice.

Another quiet night ahead, I hope. Sleeping well.

Stressless ambling. Mid Pacific

Wednesday 20

A rough and grey morning with a confused and very lumpy swell. We seem to have been going well through the night, not too far below the course and a reasonable speed, 5+, which is fine for the night hours when the priority is rest.

Morning tea and watched the breeze develop. It freshened up quite a lot about nine, so left the genoa up on its own and bore away a bit to get her closer to the course.

Cornflakes and pineapple for breakfast, boat work on the fiddle and some Spanish in the morning, usual charging with the engine etc. I will need to decant some fuel into the tank soon, but it's too rough at the moment.

Quiet afternoon, feeling down for some reason. Genoa on greens at 2100, big swell, uncomfortable. I am feeling uneasy. But good tea and chocolate pudding. Turned in at 2200, feeling sad despite all personal targets met. But nothing from Aurora. Must be a man lurking there I think.

Thursday 21
Well I woke this morning assuming it was Wednesday, but checking the calendar and the log book, it does appear to be Thursday after all.

Got tipped out of my bunk last night, a very uncomfortable rolly, noisy night with not much proper rest so feeling grumpy and depressed when I got up.

Headed up 20 degrees to try and ease the motion. Had a few cups of tea and breakfast, cornflakes and boiled eggs. Boiled one extra to have at lunch with the rest of the potato salad.

Got some work done on deck, which dispelled the blues a bit.

Folded and stowed away the no 1.

Rigged the No 4 ready to hoist, either on the pole or on the stay alone.

De-canted a jerry can of fuel into the tank, now showing ¾ full. Good job.

I need the wind to go down by 5 kts and the swell to go down with it. But a warm and sunny morning, big blue seas rolling past. Boat feeling relaxed, doing about five and a half. Stressless ambling.

Noon 134 miles. 5.6 kts, 1251 to go. Could be a week on Saturday.

Busy afternoon. Spotted monitor line frayed where it enters the down tube, the outer cover had come away altogether, so put the boat on auto and went over the stern (clipped on) and shortened both down lines so both have new bits of cover at the sheaves. The lines may be a little too thick? Also rigged a tensioner elastic to stop the slack line from jumping off the clutch sheave on the wheel.

About three it got very windy, so put up the No 4, and put the genoa away, Then it eased, so No4 down, genoa out!

The general trend seems to be for the wind to soften off a bit, which is very welcome. But I need to see the swell go as well or get itself properly organised so that I can deal with it. We go along fine for a while then along come a few big ones at the wrong angle and she gets kicked around a bit .

I want stressless ambling. Not violent rolling, creaking and clattering.

A good evening.

Friday 23

No 4 up on the pole beside the genoa, going well. Decanted two jerry cans of fresh water into the for'd tank, which has already done two weeks and changed the gas bottle, that's done two weeks as well, and re-rove the Monitor lines again. Changed a new rig for adjustments, all seemed to go ok.

Noon 127 only. Ambling right enough.

A good afternoon's sailing with the twin sails.

Some Spanish in the afternoon, but motivation waning, no word from *Shipping*. Oh dear, cynicism is creeping back in.

No. 4 down at about six, a few black clouds around, and a brief rain shower, so settled on the genoa as the overnight sail. Seems steady enough, the swell is down a bit, but still the odd bout of noisy rolling.

Evening drinks in the cockpit, learning Spanish and living on memories.

Saturday 23

Up at 0230 adjusting the genoa.

Up again at four and again at seven, No. 4 up on the pole, boat just doddering along. A busy morning; Saturday jobs, engine checks and cleaned everything in sight, sailing along slowly with the No. 4 on the pole and the genoa out full. Big container ship went past at about ten, put the vhf on, but no chat.

Noon. 122 miles ugh. Poor show, eta slipped to abt – midnight Saturday 30 and there's no point in that, since I don't want to be arriving in the dark, so it may as well slip into Sunday morning, which I am sure it will. I think there must be about a knot against us, although with the log not working it's hard to be sure, but that's just my judgment of it, looking at the way she is going through the water, and how the wake is coming off the stern. I won't be far out.

1300 No 1 up on the pole, no 4 down

Good afternoon's sailing with twin headsails. No news of Aurora on mailasail. What's going on? It's really the only fly in the ointment at the moment, and a bit sad, but there you go.

1800 no 1 down, wind shifted into the SSE at abt F4. Ok for a while then rolled genoa down to the greens, very lumpy and unpleasant motion.

Good spinach omelette for tea but it's shaping up to a very uncomfortable night with boat getting thrown around all over the place.

Sunday 24

A poor night, rolling getting kicked around, very slow, the sea and swell a bit disorganised. Boat not making the heading and getting pushed north of the track. Me unhappy.

At one stage spray came in through the small coach roof skylight and hit me in the face as I tried to sleep so I shut the skylight, but it got very stuffy so opened it again.

0800 This can't go on, creeping along, stressless ambling taken to the point where it's causing stress. Oh dear.

So No 4 up, genoa away. Main up with two reefs, wind is almost abeam, so de-powered the main so it was just giving forward drive and the boat settled into her stride. On course, doing about six and a half knots and seeming under no stress. Monitor paddle near amidships, most of the time, which is the most certain sign that everything's in harmony.

Noon. Only 126. I have been passive too long. Let's get going.

Good afternoon's sailing, on course and going well, a bit of a snooze then an hour of Spanish. It's become an act of faith.

No 4 down and genoa out on greens as the breeze seemed to be easing down quite a bit. Boat sailing well and at 2000, fifty miles from noon, good going for a change and an easy motion. Lots of small cumulus at sunset, lovely. Chicken casserole and chocolate pudding because it's so easy to make and the hot salt water you boil the bags in can be used to clean the dishes. Nothing wasted and a good double use of the energy expended to heat the water. Full stomach and a clean galley, just the right setting for a good night's sleep, I hope.

Lots of cockpit thinking time.

Monday 25

Monday again. Ah well, a bit nearer and the weather seems to have settled.

No 4 out on pole at nine, and main with two reefs. Going well.

Noon 148. Much better but 24.5 hour day due to clock shift. Still 6.3, which is good.

1500 N04 down, no1 up on pole with the main.

1800 No.1 down, black clouds and squalls.

Saw a white light on the port bow at around nine. Could be Duetto?

Settled on genoa on greens and two reefs for the night, gong well, good steady motion.

Tuesday 26

At 0300 the white light had gone. At daylight there was no sign of a sail. Set the No 1 on the pole and left the genoa up so was sailing with both jibs and the main. Got a bit exciting so rolled away the genoa. Good sailing all morning with the No1 and the main. Wind came round into the south a bit so making the course. Hot and sunny.

Noon, 133 miles. 5.5, a wee bit disappointing. Still, looks good for late Sat /Sun morning.

Struggling with Spanish for 'that, these, those'. The words are so similar and my capacity to commit things to memory is so degraded that I really had a job with it. It's an effort to make myself learn so I stand in the cockpit, point at things or a thing, and utter what I hope are the right words. There's not much harm in it I suppose.

Reading Stephen Fry's autobiography. Oh to have a brain like that.

Thursday 28

At about three this morning a flying fish came through the hatch or the skylight, and hit me in the face. I woke and thought something had rolled off the galley and I can usually identify the item by its distinctive noise even in the dark. But this was a new one. On went the light and there it was, fully grown in peak condition, flapping around on the cabin sole between the galley and the chart table. My first thought was 'well that will do for breakfast' but I was still half-asleep and couldn't face killing and gutting it there and then and I didn't want to put it into the fridge alive in case it took fright and crapped on the tortillas. I picked it up and returned it, still flapping, to its natural element. What a tale it must have had to tell its chums: 'I was in this strange floating thing with a giant from Scotland', Aye right, whatever you say.

Made mosquito screens for the opening ports in the cockpit and generally tidied in the morning. Sailing well with the genoa and the main; on course, good speed.

Noon 147 very good. We need to keep up six knots. If we do Saturday evening is still a possibility but realistically we are looking at Sunday morning, maybe slowing down over the last twelve hours for a morning arrival. There's no point in messing around trying to anchor in the dark and anyway, I want to see the islands as we approach.

Going well in the early evening, maybe getting out of the current a bit.

Friday 29

Rain squall and totally overcast at sunrise so a grey morning. A bit of sun about nine but not much otherwise. No 1 up on the pole, sailing well.

Big cleaning session in and around the cockpit, all the cubby hole lockers cleaned out what a load of crap I found. There were old bits of everything plus an oil can I hadn't seen in ages. Noon. 143 miles, but 24.5 hrs. So 5.8, still ok.

No 1 down, then pole down. Hanked on the No 4 and set it.

Gybed at about 1400. We were well south of the line.

A strange afternoon, grey with lumps. A few rain showers but not too much wind in them so enjoyed an all over wash in the cockpit. Then one arrived, with plenty of wind, just as I had poured my happy hour beer so I had to get into action. Dropped the main and sailed with the No 4, but it wasn't enough area so No 4 down and genoa out. Going along fine on Stbd. gybe, heading north of west, at about five knots but that's fine. She can carry on all night like this and we will have worked our way north of the line again by the morning, plus, no strain on boat or me (I hope.)

Tinned sausages, mashed potato and Bisto/ Oxo gravy mix for tea. Not exactly sophisticated, but very tasty.

Friday 29

Grey lumpy, fairly windy and wet. Rain squall came through at 6.30am so in went the genoa and up went the number four. No morning tea in the sun this morning as there is no sun. Feeling really grumpy and down this morning so shaved off the beard. It was getting to be just an itchy nuisance and I don't need a crop of white hair growing out of my chin to remind me that I am getting on. Felt a bit better.

Sailed all morning in the grey and gusty stuff with some big lumps of sea rolling up behind and no real break in the clouds. Very uncomfortable with the sea all over the place and the boat getting thrown about.

Noon 126 for the day, 233 to go. Sunday afternoon, no sooner I think. A very uncomfortable afternoon and I feel really uneasy - a bit like a tightrope walker who has almost managed to cross the Grand Canyon, then notices that his shoelace has come undone. I will be being very, very careful over the next couple of days. Please, whoever is in charge of these things just let me get there in one piece.

I have done the philosophising under the stars, the beard growing and all the other stuff. I am tired of having to hang on every time I move around and I have run out of interesting things to eat. I would kill for a plate of roast lamb and a pint and a bag of crisps.

It's time for a rest.

Saturday 30

Up at 0630, fine blue sky. The crappy stuff seems to have gone through. Tea in the sun at 7am, great, some time to think and look ahead. Set full genoa and No 4 on the pole at 7.30am, good sailing all morning, then got gusty at 1100 so no 4 down, genoa alone for a while. Did some washing. Saturday engine checks etc.

Noon 122, not too bad considering the quiet night (easy on the crew) 122 to go. Tomorrow afternoon, fingers crossed.

Good sailing all afternoon. Slept for an hour, woke up and lay in the bunk thinking about the trip. I began to feel much more positive for some reason and started to think about all the improvements I had worked on the boat since I got her, and some of the things I would still like to do, and all the time and cash I had invested in her. Looking at it that way it would seem crazy to sell the boat in NZ, particularly with the new engine, rudder repair, new headsails. I would just be giving it all away to some lucky guy and would be left without a boat. So I got to thinking about next year and what I would do, probably cruising NZ until May, then make up my mind about the rest of the year. But there are the imponderables. No word from Aurora what on earth is going on? The last message was so positive and loving, then silence for a fortnight. That's a big consideration for the future as well but not if there's no future in it.

Not sure what to make of it.

But back to the present. Arrival in Polynesia tomorrow. Fingers crossed, slowing down tonight a bit so that I see the land at first light and can enjoy the approach, hopefully getting into the Bay in the early afternoon. A few birds flying around so must be a good sign.

76 miles to go at 1900. Sea Me has picked up a signal but I can't see anything on the horizon. Not unusual, it often is the case. Still, seems there is someone else around. Boil in the bag chicken casserole and chocolate pudding which is the lazy man's perfect dinner. Many more stars tonight, swell down a bit, boat sailing well. All clean dry and tidy below. Galley gleaming. No more instant coffee though and the cafetiere uses too much water, bad planning. I will make a proper pot of coffee in the morning. My last night at sea for a while and an occasion to be savoured I think. Let's hope it all goes smoothly. Almost there.

On the morning of May 1, the outline of Hive Oa began to emerge from the haze. A noon I had just eight miles to go and by two in the afternoon I was at anchor, with a stern anchor as well to hold the boat head into the swell which rolled relentlessly in to the bay. But uncomfortable or not, I had arrived. I had sailed just over 3000 miles from the Galapagos, the longest solo passage I had ever made. Time for safe arrival drinks and lots and lots of rest.

10

The

Marquesas

Making Friends with the Locals

THE swell rolls relentlessly into the wooded bay at Autona and all the boats set stern anchors to hold themselves bow into it. There is better shelter closer in to the jetty but that area has to be kept clear for the ferry so the yachts cluster on the other side. It certainly was not a good anchorage.

Almost every day cloud would build up around the mountain that overlooks the bay. After a few hours it would start to blow and then rain. For half an hour or so the rain would pour down in torrents, then suddenly stop as the cloud cleared to reveal a magnificent rainbow stretching from one side of the bay to the other. Soaked and steaming in the sun the boats would roll in the swell and the cycle would start over. I had hardly worn the deck shoes I had bought in Curacao, preferring to sail barefoot but now I had to put them on and walk the mile or so over the hill into town to check in with Customs and Immigration. The shoes hurt and it wasn't long before I had blisters on both heels. Walking into town was painful but walking back when the Gendarmerie told me to come back the next day was even worse.

I called at the Post Office to see if I could get online but there was a power cut and no-one seemed sure of when it would be restored. It was apparently a regular occurrence and didn't seem to matter in the general scheme of things. On the way back I stopped at a restaurant up on the hill above the road and treated myself to lunch. The steak arrived at my table on the veranda along with the flies, who did their best to completely cover the meat. I have never seen so many flies trying to get onto one plate at one time. It looked as if someone had sprinkled raisins over the food. So I ate with the fork in one hand and used the other to swipe and flap at the flies. Somehow the edge had gone off my appetite.

I was about to receive news that would put a big smile back on my face. My daughter, Anna, whom as far as I knew was in Paris, e-mailed to ask if I would be going anywhere near an island called Ahe, near Tahiti, she thought. I got the charts out but at first I couldn't find it. Then on a much larger scale chart spotted it - a flyspeck of an atoll on the paper, a few hundred miles north east of Tahiti.

Ever the free spirit, Anna had quit her job in Paris and was heading out to the atoll to work on a pearl farm. I had long since stopped being surprised by anything my children did but this was even more out of the ordinary than usual.

Was there a pass into the reef? Was there anywhere to anchor? Could I get in? Yes. Great Anna, see you there.

The French painter Gaugin lived here and spent his time painting and living in his legendary House Of Love with a collection of local ladies. Eventually, his lifestyle killed him and he is buried above the town, presumably still smiling. There wasn't a great deal of interaction between the yachts but I spent some time with a French couple on their way back from America to their home in Tahiti, where they owned a night club and they were able to give me a very useful insight into life in Polynesia. They had sailed thousands and thousands of miles in their boat *Pacha* and they were good company.

I spent my 65th birthday alone on board, a condition I was becoming accustomed to. A celebration stew and a bottle of red wine helped and the next day I sailed a few miles over to the island of Tahuata and anchored in the bay where it blew hard. Like all the Marquesas, Tahuata is very mountainous and heavily-wooded and the bay we were in was pretty much deserted. There were a few other boats there and one evening, after we had been snorkelling, we all went ashore and had a barbeque. It should have been enjoyable but for some reason I didn't feel well and, in the middle of the night, I woke up with a severe pain my chest. I tried to get back to sleep hoping that it would go away but it didn't. With my history of high blood pressure and stroke I began to worry that it could be something serious. By the middle of the day I had had enough and set off to sail the hundred miles to Baie Tiohae on Nuku Hiva where I knew there was a hospital.

I got in the next morning, reported myself to the Gendarmerie and set off to the hospital. I hate hospitals but I was feeling bad and very worried. In these situations my mind always goes straight to the worst possible scenario and I wondered what I would do if I wound up being admitted and they said I wasn't fit enough to sail the boat.

The hospital, a one-storey building with shady verandas surrounded by trees, had a very peaceful air about it. I explained the situation and was soon lying on a spotless white sheet in an immaculate examination room with a kindly French nurse taking my history and listening to my story. I felt like some sort of penniless vagrant in my faded T shirt and torn shorts as she took my blood pressure and attached the contacts for the ECG. Slowly I began to relax and almost looked forward to the possibility of spending a few days being cared for and fed in these restful surroundings. With the assessment completed, I sat in a comfortable chair on the veranda enjoying the cool breeze and waiting for the doctor to look over my results. I began to realise how much I had been missing basic comforts like the comfortable chair but most of all conversation and human company.

After a while I was called in and had a chat with the young French doctor who was on duty. He was a keen sailor from Brittany and very interested in my voyage. After a while the conversation turned to my health. I was underweight but my ECG was normal and my BP only slightly raised. The pain in my chest, which was already starting to feel better, had been gastric in origin and I must not worry.

Walking down the dusty road to the harbour I began to see that sailing the boat and coping with the weather were only a small part of the story. My new life was a far cry from my previous one in a serviced apartment in

Seoul, with dinners in restaurants and life in an office and I was turning into a different person. But if the process was to reach a successful conclusion I would have to start trying to look after myself better. Being lean and mean was one thing, becoming completely knackered was another. It would be a great pity if it turned out that I was able to handle the boat and sail it tens of thousands of miles across the oceans but couldn't even keep myself in good shape.

With the worry of chest pain out of the way I began to explore a bit and walked round the shore most mornings. Dogs seem to roam at will in most Pacific islands and every day I would see a couple of groups, usually five or six, sauntering along the road like a bunch of lads on a Saturday morning. They were just wandering along and sniffing around to see what they could get up to. Although groups of dogs are not a usual sight at home, here it was normal and they seemed to mean no harm whatsoever. One evening I was sitting on the shore and looking out across the bay and one of the pack came along and sat down beside me. It was quite touching. I was finally mixing with the locals.

At the boat landing a German lady had a small food van serving crepes and ice cream. She lived on the island with her Marquesan husband and her small child and most days I would stop by and enjoy a crepe and some coffee. Often I would see locals on horseback with just a blanket for a saddle and a very primitive rope bridle. They are great horsemen and go up into the mountains for days on end with their dogs to hunt goat and pig.

The Marquesas were the last stronghold of cannibalism in the Pacific and I occasionally heard dark tales of its continuing in the more remote areas. At the time I had no idea whether there was any substance to them. However, I later heard that not long after my visit there had, in fact, been an incident in which a tourist had lost his life. It was a chilling thought.

In the evening the fishing boats would come in to the dock, strangely designed with the helmsman's cockpit at the bow, and steered by a vertical tiller which moved side to side like the joystick of an aircraft. The tuna were landed and gutted on stone tables at the water's edge with all the unwanted bits simply being thrown back into the water. The sharks were well used to this and would gather in anticipation then thrash around wildly competing for the food as soon as the first scrap of bloodied meat hit the water. The locals didn't seem bothered but they weren't commuting back and forward in small rubber dinghies the way we were. I didn't like the look of it at all.

But the general air was one of laid-back indolence. The few administrative buildings around the harbour were neat and well kept, like the hospital, even the jail had flowers round the windows and a close-cut lawn in front of it. The inmates were usually allowed out each day to keep the gardens looking good and to do other community-based work around the village. With three meals a day, plus a little light gardening, conditions in the clink were probably a lot better than they would have enjoyed at home.

One day I sailed around to Daniel's Bay a few miles to the west and anchored in the amphitheatre-like surroundings with mountains towering on all sides. At night, with no shore light pollution and a clear sky, it was like looking up at the stars through the roof of a huge stadium with the floodlights off. It was truly beautiful and completely silent. In the mornings, anchored in the bay, I would hear cocks crowing and dogs barking in the village and wood smoke would drift out over the quiet water. These sounds were to become pleasantly familiar as I visited other islands and will always now conjure up images of the Pacific.

Daniel's Bay is famous in cruising history. Everyone who is anyone, from Pidgeon through Hiscock to the present day cruising gurus has been there. They have signed the log book, given Daniel a gift, usually a tin of spam which he loved and collected their mountain pure water from his spring whilst being pestered by the infamous No No's, whose bites invariably became infected. After years of midge-infested evenings in Scottish lochs, I knew what to expect and wasn't too bothered.

The ruins of Daniel's old home are still there but Daniel himself has long since gone to his reward, seemingly taking his log books with him which is sad. Still, it saved me handing out a tin of spam. However, I did go ashore in the dinghy, just before high water, and negotiated the sandbar getting up stream in the creek and filling my jerry cans with the fabled liquid. Not a sign, sound or suspicion of a No, No. None. I know single handers are regarded with a certain sense of suspicion by the rest of the cruising community, but when even the infamous black flies of the Marquesas wouldn't come and have nibble I wondered if, perhaps, it was time to review my personal freshness strategy.

The days went by pleasantly enough. I got to know the lady with the van and made my daily walk along the shore, occasionally meeting up with sailors from other boats, all making their way across this mighty ocean in time with the seasons and nearly all heading for Tahiti. I was disappointed to be hearing so little from Aurora, but looking forward hugely to meeting up with Anna, a week or so further down the line. Since it was very unlikely that I would ever be back, I wanted to visit another of the islands before I left. I sailed over to Ua Pou and anchored in the bay. I was on my own again. The bay wasn't particularly sheltered and the boat rolled around in the swell. There was no sign of life on the shore but I had already stowed the dinghy anyway so I wasn't bothered about not going ashore. I felt a bit guilty about not doing more exploring but it isn't much fun doing it on your own anyway.

Beyond rolled and snatched at her chain sheering about in the gusts that came down from the massive peaks, their tops hidden in cloud. I began to feel really uneasy about the 450 mile passage across to Manihi, but had no idea why. There was a steady 20 kts of breeze forecast for the whole trip, which would be around the upper level of the comfort zone, but that shouldn't pose any real problems. Goodness knows I had covered enough miles in similar conditions by now, so why was I so restless? Who knows? Maybe it had all been a little too easy so far.

With the passage set to take three and a half days I didn't want to leave until late afternoon to give a morning arrival in Manihi so I had the day to fill. During the morning I got the boat ready and did some tidying and securing. I even looked over the contents of the grab bag and put in some additional fishing gear and a spare pair of specs. I called Aurora on the sat phone. She was in mid-Atlantic and having a tough time of it and was resting down below when I called but it was good to talk to her. She sounded very positive, although she had had her share of hard weather, and was currently waiting for more to arrive. She was a tough woman. So what was spooking me? I had no idea. By early afternoon I had had enough of killing time and, when a really unpleasant squall arrived with the usual heavy rain, I decided to get out straight away and hove up and set off. Once clear of the land the breeze steadied up but it was certainly fresh, so I left the main down and flew the genoa, first on greens then full on, then on greens again. As the evening came in the breeze freshened again so I set the number four on the inner stay and rolled away the genoa for the night. It stayed rolled away for the rest of the trip.

It was a rough night but the new monitor lines were working well and she steered beautifully down the swells.

There certainly was a big enough sea and the wind was well above the 20 knots forecast. I was getting 20 apparent and every so often a difficult sea out-of-step with the rest would chuck the stern around bringing the wind onto the beam and increasing the apparent to around 25 knots until she got back on track.

I had to hold on constantly. Even boiling the kettle was something of an effort. I felt down and uneasy. There was no fun in it. The small misfortunes began the second night out.

After the evening meal of stew, taken from a bowl rather than a plate, I went to empty some left-overs over the side. The bowl was the only one of its size on board, an old friend, but my hand was greasy and when *Beyond* took a lurch, as I reached over the toe rail, the potatoes and gravy landed on the side deck and the bowl went for a swim. I hate breaking or losing things and it made me feel even worse.

Another rough night followed. The light rain coming in through the hatch wasn't heavy or steady enough to warrant putting in the boards but it was wet enough to make the cabin sole slippery. At about three in the morning I was awakened by the noise of some plates sliding about in a locker. I knew exactly which locker to open, and I was dressed anyway, so I didn't bother to put a light on. As she began to roll to port I slid the locker open but she lurched back to starboard and there was a crash in the dark as my Pyrex cafetiere shot out of the locker, hit the deck and shattered - another old friend gone. What was worse I was now sliding around on the wet cabin sole in the dark, in bare feet, with a lot of broken glass scattered around. I held on tight to the pillar and managed to get a light on and find some sandals. That cafetiere had been the centrepiece of a little coffee ritual enjoyed in fine weather, or in port, when at 10.30 each morning, weather permitting, I would sit down and take the time to really enjoy a great cup of ground coffee, instead of the hastily mixed mugs of instant I was usually reduced to. I was angry and very unhappy. What on earth was going on? The motion was bad, the boat felt uneasy and what should have been a stroll downwind was turning into quite a test of patience. Pacific? I didn't think so.

I scooped up as much of the glass as I could see. Reaching out through the hatch, I threw it up to leeward. I should have known better. Several pieces hit the solar panel and fell back into the cockpit so I now had broken glass there as well. No more bare feet for me for a while.

My confidence had taken a knock. Knowing things like this come in threes I started to be particularly careful in everything I did. With the number four up and drawing I was quite glad there was no need to leave the cockpit at all. On the afternoon of the third day I backed the jib to slow the boat down to a sedate four knots and we carried on for the rest of that day and the following night with the seas rolling up behind and surging past. I tried some video, but as usual, the filmed version didn't really reflect the reality.

I raised the low reef of Manihi at a distance of eight miles just after breakfast. This was my first atoll, with its low-lying fringing reef and palms bent over by the wind. No mountains here, just coral patches, weathered palms and sand. There is often a strong current running in the passes into these atolls and I motored in feeling very nervous. There was still time for misfortune number three. But I got down to the south end where *Pacha* and *Endorphin*, friends from the Marquesas, were already lying and I anchored in 17 metres, which is about as deep as I can manage.

The boat was steady for the first time in days and I was tired but at least I was there. The next day I sailed for Ahe, to meet up with Anna.

11

The Simple Life

THE wind was from right astern and it wasn't worth setting any sail for the short distance to Ahe so I motored over and coasted down the west side of the reef, picking out the pass and coming in with the tide behind me.

Safely through the pass I turned and headed slowly south. Shortly a big aluminium dory approached, bouncing over the waves. There in the stern sat Anna, whom I hadn't seen since Portugal nine months ago. She looked even more beautiful than I remembered and I felt a surge of paternal pride seeing her there, hair blowing in the wind, tanned, and smiling and clearly in her element. The dory was being driven by a very large, bronzed and tattooed guy and I was led down towards a partially wrecked white hut sitting in stilts on a coral patch. We circled round the leeward side, a line was passed up which I made fast, then added another of my own to form a bridle which let the boat lie swinging to leeward of the shoal. 'What am I going to do when the tide changes or the wind shifts'? I asked. I was assured that the current always runs one way and the wind would not shift until September.

I was still uneasy but the crew climbed aboard and we spent a relaxing hour catching up. It's not often you meet up with your daughter, who just happens to be living in a hut on stilts attached to a pearl farm in a lagoon in the middle of the Pacific Ocean - but there we were and it was great to see her again. Later we went ashore to the farm for a meal and to meet the other guys. Anna was the only girl there.

It was a long ride back to the boat that night and I still worried about the unorthodox mooring but, thankfully, as predicted, the wind remained steady. Although I was on the leeward side of the lagoon, with a fetch of several miles, the coral on which the hut stood broke the worst of the seas. *Beyond* lay sedately in its lee swinging quietly on her lines.

One dark night there was a particularly harsh rain squall and we swung around and heeled in the initial blast of wind which preceded the rain. I got up into the cockpit and started the engine ready to slip and run if things got difficult but, thankfully, everything held and I was saved the embarrassment of having to write a letter to the insurance company, starting: 'I was moored to the stilts of a hut in Tuamotus.'

I spent a week at the farm in Kamoka, joining in some of the work and the recreation where, in return for my efforts as an unskilled oyster scraper, I ate a delicious lunch each day usually of freshly-speared fish, rice and some salad. The guys on the farm work hard from early each morning for very little reward. In some ways it's an idyllic existence but it's a very physical one with a lot of free diving involved to recover the nets of oysters and re set the buoys. They were all very fit and swam like fish. Anna has always been a good athlete and I was very proud when one of the guys told me she was the first visiting worker to join fully in every aspect of the work actually getting involved in the diving and underwater stuff.

One evening after work was finished we headed out to the pass for some spear fishing, anchored against the setting sun the dory provided a steady base. With five experts in the water there was soon a good collection of fish flapping in the bottom of the boat. I got into the water to watch but stayed a safe distance from the action. The light began to go and we headed back to the farm under a red and darkening sky, cleaning the fish on the way. We then enjoying the kind of meal you would have paid a fortune for in a restaurant, washed down with rum and lime juice drunk from a selection of chipped glasses and jam jars. Golden days indeed.

At the end of the week the boys from the farm came out on board for a few beers. My French seemed to become more fluent as the drinks went down and we yarned and laughed long into the evening. The next day I headed three miles down to the village to anchor inside the reef where I would have access to the small store and post office.

Nearing the reef I went up to get the anchor ready. Because *Beyond*'s anchor didn't easily stow on the roller, I keep it on deck with the chain led over the pulpit. This means that when you want to get it ready for lowering you need to lift it over the rail and transfer the weight to the windlass. I don't like putting a shock load on the gypsy so I usually lower the anchor over the rail using the boathook, letting the weight come gently onto the chain. It's a bit of a struggle in anything of a sea but it was absolutely flat calm. It should have been easy so I just held onto the chain with my left hand, lifted the anchor over the pulpit with my right, and let go of it.

As Homer Simpson would say – Doh.

I had my left hand too close to the stem head roller and, when the weight came on the chain, my thumb came into immediate and painful contact with the sharp edge of the side plate which neatly sliced the top of it open, just under the nail which folded back pouring blood. I danced back to the cockpit, dripping red everywhere and in some real pain. I wrapped the damaged digit in kitchen towel too frightened to look closely at what I had done. Besides, the boat was doing four knots on the auto pilot towards the first of the reef beacons and I had to get her anchored.

With *Beyond* safely at anchor I took a close look at my little problem. The nail was as good as detached, wobbling around on what was left of the flesh underneath. I had no TCP left so I dipped the whole mess in a solution of bleach and hot salt water and let it soak for a while, then taped it all back together again, smeared on some Savlon and hoped for the best. It was not a procedure I had covered at the First Aid Course.

My thumb was pounding so I awarded myself a couple of pain killers and a cold beer and hoped for the best. It bled all night.

The next few days were painful and awkward to say the least. The thumb took a long time to stop oozing blood but I had started a course of penicillin to avoid any sort of infection and gradually the end of my thumb closed up again. It was only then that I realised that this was the third and worst of my three misfortunes. I sincerely hoped the spell had been lifted. I had a limited number of thumbs.

I stayed in behind the reef for a week with Anna on board resting my thumb and waiting for some very windy weather to go through. I made a protective cage for the thumb out of strips cut from a beer can, epoxy and glass cloth. It looked very professional and worked well. As the week went on more boats arrived to shelter; one whose in-mast mainsail stowage system had failed, and who had spent a very unpleasant couple of days in thirty knots of wind with his sail stuck two thirds out. He had steered by hand until the weather had quietened down enough for his crew to go up the mast and pass some lines round the sail. He was glad to get in. A lovely American boat, *Chesapeake*, also arrived but being last in had a job finding enough room in amongst the coral to anchor. We met them ashore one evening and they came aboard for a drink. Great people and I later got to know them well.

On the Thursday the stores ship from Tahiti arrived and for a few hours the pier became the focal point of activity for the whole atoll, with small boats arriving from the outlying motus to collect freight and to take advantage of the chance to sit on the pier with friends and catch up with news. The Polynesians are very sociable people and the arrival of the boat provided the ideal excuse for a gathering. Friends from the farm arrived as well to pick up stores that had been sent from Tahiti and some sheets of timber. They came aboard and we sat in the cockpit with the cool evening breeze blowing through the anchorage and the friendly stars looking down. Beers were drunk and goodbyes said yet again and very late the dory set off for the farm a couple of miles away in the dark. Two days later we sailed out of the lagoon and set a course for Tahiti, 300 miles to the west. But we didn't leave empty-handed. As we motored up past Kamoka, the dory came bouncing out in a cloud of spray and came close alongside to throw up a parcel of fresh fish and a gift for Anna. I had only been at Ahe for two weeks but I had fallen under its spell and I was sorry to say goodbye to such great people. I can only guess how Anna must have felt and I deliberately didn't look in her direction as we motored out of the pass. We had an easy trip over, arriving off the entrance to the harbour at Papeete late in the afternoon and motoring in to moor at the marina right in the heart of the town. Within the space of a couple of days we had moved from a very basic life on a low-lying coral atoll to the very heart of what was once the jewel in the crown of colonial France.

12

Tahiti and the Islands

Island Hopping in Paradise

AT the end of his wonderful book, "The Long Way" Bernard Moitessier describes being moored along with a small band of like-minded sailing vagabonds in the same spot as that in which *Beyond* now lay. He decries the fact that the trees are being cut down and the grass torn up to make way for the three lane highway being built along the shore, raging against the tyranny of the machines that were destroying everything in their path. He tells of how he and his friends are gradually pushed further and further down the harbour until they remain, clinging to the last vestiges of green, a sad and angry bunch of ocean sailors sidelined by progress and seemingly powerless to do anything about it.

I wish he could see it now. The highway is still there, of course, and it is crowded with traffic at the rush hour, but unlike traffic in a European city where rush hour is a stressful experience, the traffic here seems laid back and almost quiet. It's also opulent. There are supposed to be more Porche Cayenne's per head of population in

Papeete than in any other city in the world which I suppose is a reasonable indicator of prosperity. But even these mighty beasts ease to a halt and let you over the crossings. Drivers smile and nod making the experience somehow relaxed.

The old quay area, where the cruising boats used to lie, stern to has been re-vamped and the shore is occupied by a beautiful park with many trees and acres of beautifully tended grass. There is a path at the very edge of the shore and in the early morning joggers and walkers by the score pass along it to savour the sights and scents of the ocean before beginning their day. At the weekend families come and enjoy the peace and children play amongst the trees. Even walking through the area on my way to and from the supermarket was a pleasant and relaxing experience.

We stayed in Papeete for a week, with the boat connected to shore power and with fresh water on tap and the ability to step ashore, we felt as if we had a suite at the Ritz. Just across the road downtown Papeete waited to be explored.

The town itself had a worldly and cosmopolitan air with expensive restaurants, bars and jewellers by the dozen, all selling black pearls. Two blocks back smaller stores, many of them Chinese owned, thrive and there is a wonderful under-cover market selling every kind of local food imaginable with fish so fresh it's almost still flapping on the slab.

By night the restaurants cater to the tourists and the cruise ship trade. At the weekend many featured small bands playing a mixture of local and imported sounds on ukuleles and guitars. During the day little groups of street musicians would gather and sit around playing and singing for passing pedestrians. But it certainly was not all opulence.

Two blocks further west, in sharp contrast to the music and cocktail hour atmosphere of the downtown bars and shops, a selection of the town's less fortunate souls sleep on the pavement under the trees surrounded by bundles of their possessions and the usual collection of stray dogs and chickens while cockroaches, the size of clockwork toys, scuttle around amongst them. Round the corner a selection of rather bedraggled-looking girls clutch their fags and phones and wait for custom. Street life in paradise.

After a week we moved down the lagoon, past the end of the airport runway, and anchored off Marina Tiana, along with about another 70 cruising boats, some of which had clearly been there for a long time. There was contrast again here, with the locals living in squalid and filthy conditions in disintegrating huts at the water's edge. Only 500 metres away the fabulous yachts of the massively wealthy lay stern to, gleaming in the sun, their towering masts looking down imperiously at the shore and onto the collection of low budget, or in some cases, no budget cruisers anchored to seaward. The locals must occasionally wonder if they really do live in paradise.

Beside the dock with its row of super yachts the 'Pink Coconut' bar waited to suck up any money left in the sailors' pockets. The staff at the bar must have trained at 'Shelter Bay' or perhaps they could spot the slightly hard up and unlikely to tip folk amongst the more glamorous and well-heeled of their clientele. One evening they put on a happy hour. With the prices reduced from the absurd to the merely infuriating the bar was mobbed, with everyone going hard at it to maximise their short term advantage. It was good fun, regardless, and there were many very interesting people around.

Late one afternoon an American from the boat closest to us in the anchorage went by in his dinghy and seeing that we were Scots, told us that he played the bagpipes every evening at 5.30. "When you see the sun set behind the mountains over on Moorea," he said, "Listen for the pipes." How kind.

As sunset approached we looked wistfully to the hills and, sure enough, right on cue the strains of Amazing Grace came floating over from the other boat. Amateur bag pipe playing can sometimes be a little harsh on the ear but this man could certainly play. We were both really touched. Neither of us had been home in a long time and there's nothing quite like the sound of the pipes to stir the emotions of the Scots overseas. To hear them played so well, right at sunset in such a wonderful setting, filled our hearts.

The moment lost some of its magic when, after the first passage of melody, there was a prolonged roll of side drums and the complete band joined in. It was a recording. But the overall effect was therapeutic and we laughed even more the following evening when the process was repeated whilst our musical neighbour was still on deck working at the bow of his boat. Not only was it a recording, it was on a timer.

In Papeete we met up with Paul, a yachting professional I had first met briefly in Auckland a few years previously. A well-known figure in NZ sailing, a professional diver and all-round great guy, he is one of the most helpful people I know and certainly knew his way around the shore side sailing scene. We were talking about anti-fouling one evening at anchor and the next morning I heard some strange sounds coming from outside the hull. There was a smart white launch moored alongside with no-one in it. Paul had come over with his dive gear and was under the hull. He scrubbed the whole thing then called back later and took Anna off for some snorkelling. It was all very good fun.

After a few days we sailed the short distance over to Moorea, anchoring firstly in Cooks Bay and then in Opunohu Bay, both truly beautiful locations. I had been reading Cook's diaries on the way across the Pacific and it was quite a thrill to anchor in the same places as I had read about. Surrounded by heavily-wooded mountains, these bays are sparsely populated with just a few huts set back in the trees. Every morning we would hear the now familiar sound of crowing cockerels and barking dogs. The shores on which we gazed were probably exactly as Cook saw them so long ago. It was a strange feeling. Apart from the pleasure of her company, having Anna on board was proving to be very helpful. Almost every day some bronzed and immaculately-clad guy from one of the super yachts would come by just to see if I needed anything. How kind. "No", I would reply. "Everything's fine, thanks". No sign of the kind gentleman leaving. "Is Anna aboard?" he would ask. Strangely enough although all of these beautiful craft had lady crew members none ever made an appearance.

Moorea

From Moorea we sailed overnight to Huahine, another beautiful island about 100 miles to the northwest and anchored in behind the reef. The swell breaking on the reef was impressive and added to the beauty of our surroundings. One evening I rowed over to another British yacht to say hello and they kindly invited us over for a drink. Mike and Katherine on *Falbala* became great friends and, happily, I was able to meet up with them again in Tonga then later in New Zealand. The places I was visiting were memorable but some of the people I was meeting were just as good to know. It's possibly the fact that cruising people share a common interest and, in many cases, have visited the same place, but their company was always entertaining. I have spent many a memorable evening with other sailors yarning long into the night.

The forecast was for a few days of unsettled weather. As the swell in the lagoon began to build we moved round into a nearby bay. On the way Mike managed to get a line around his prop. Good sailor as he was there was not enough wind to sail up to the anchor so we towed him in with two dinghies amongst a great deal of joking and conflicting advice. With the anchor down Anna put her free diving skills to good use and went down to clear the prop.

Mike was worried about the length of time she was under but I knew that, even just on breath, she could go a lot deeper than she was and stay a lot longer. After what seemed an age, up she came with the bits of the rope in her hand and a big smile on her face. *Falbala* was bigger than *Beyond* and a very well equipped boat so Anna went below to enjoy a hot shower, the first in many days.

I wanted to replace the main down shaft bearings on the steering pedestal so we moved on to Raiatea where I knew there was French-run boatyard to do the job. It took a couple of days and there was a rather strange atmosphere about the place but they seemed to know what they were doing and we got the work completed. The French love double chine steel built cruising boats and the Pacific is littered with examples, some of them built by their owners. Not all amateur builders get it right and the yard had a few shockers up on blocks, some of which looked as if they wouldn't be going much further. With the work completed we sailed on to Bora Bora. It was a beautiful sail and I felt a great sense of pride to be sailing into this famous lagoon beneath the twin peaks of the mountains. To make the day complete the New Zealand *Beyond* lay peacefully at anchor, having arrived a week or so earlier.

Anna and I were getting on well and enjoying our time together in the islands and Bora Bora is one of the most beautiful. The town is a few kilometres from the Yacht Club and still retained a village atmosphere. The people were charming, the sun shone, and we made the most of it walking into town nearly every day. We were there at the time of the local festival at which teams from the island competed with each other in song and dance. The main event was held in the evenings and the crowds gathered round the sand arena to cheer on their favourites, whilst the thirsty amongst them added moral support from their refuge in the thatched bars around the perimeter. Everyone who was anyone was there to watch the judges decide which team from the island would go forward to the final in Tahiti.

There used to be a tradition in these islands that the youngest male of a family was raised as a girl and kept home with his sisters whilst his older brothers went off to war with other islands. To a certain extent that tradition persists today although the wars have declined in popularity.

When grown up these guys mix happily with their mates, distinctive only by their feminine characteristics, their grace of movement and sometimes their manner of dress. One evening John, from the other *Beyond,* and I had taken a break from watching the dancing and dropped in to one of the ring side tents for a beer. At the bar a statuesque local guy, well over six feet tall, heavily muscled and tattooed, was flouncing around in a pink cocktail dress and swinging a small handbag, the life and soul of the party. I was facing the bar but John, the archetypical straight Kiwi, had his back to it and was finding it hard not to look around and see what was going on. "John," I said. "Don't look round now, I don't want to alarm you but that guy seems to have taken a fancy to you". It was the first time I had seen a New Zealander abandon a half-finished beer.

With all the time I had already spent in the Galapagos and the other Pacific Islands and, after the thousands of miles I had sailed in these waters, I was beginning to feel like a true voyager. For a time I had been thinking about getting a small tattoo, both as a mark of my life long association with the sea and also to mark my voyage to Polynesia. Tattoos have always been a big part of Pacific culture and there is a very strong movement to keep the culture alive so there is no shortage of opportunities to get one. I looked at a few designs but even the simplest seemed very elaborate and far too big to me. I wanted something small and original. Anna and I talked it over one evening and we decided that we would each design a small tattoo, which we would have done on our left feet, as a memento of our mid Pacific father and daughter reunion. I drew a small fish with a smile on its face and took it along to the tattoo man. At first his artistic sensibilities were offended. Why would I want anything as silly as that and on my foot? Why couldn't I have one of his traditional tribal designs? To start with I wanted something unique to me and small, reasoning that the cost and pain of getting the job done would be related to size and complexity of the design. Anyway, it was my foot and my money. After a while he swallowed his pride and agreed so the next day I turned up and sat down while he got on with the job. I was glad it was small, because there is very little flesh just back from your toes and it was as sore as hell. Added to this he clearly took great pride in his work, would not be rushed and kept going over some bits of it again.

It was a bit like having a bread knife drawn across your foot. But eventually he finished. I had strict instructions to keep my little masterpiece out of the sun and away from water for ten days. I set off back to the boat where I proudly showed my indelible souvenir to Anna.

"Was it sore, Dad?", she inquired. "No, not very", I lied.

The next day Anna went along with her more elaborate design which met with more approval from the tattoo man. She arrived back on board later in the morning with the rather shaken air of someone who has just endured a long and painful procedure at the dentist. "Dad, you must have a very high pain threshold," she said. I said nothing. My pain threshold is very low but I could hardly have walked out with half a fish tattooed on my foot.

We must have presented a strange picture over the next few days each wearing one sock and puttering around in the dinghy with our left feet stuck up in the air to keep them dry but we came to love our little mementoes and still do.

But time was passing and I had to get Anna to Rarotonga in the Cook Islands to catch her flight back home where she was due to go back to university for a Master's year. So in mid-July we started getting the boat ready for sea again and began saying goodbye to the people we had met during our time in the islands. It's a small world for sailors and, rather than say any kind of long term farewells, cruising people usually just say: "See you down the line." It often works out that way.

We kept an eye on the weather and finally lifted the anchor and sailed out through the reef on July 19, chased out to sea ahead of a fierce rainsquall which came down from the mountain to see us off. We set off sailing fast to the southwest and before long Bora Bora had faded out of sight behind the clouds.

BORA BORA TO TONGA

The trip over from Bora Bora was slow with light winds all the way and we had to do a lot of motoring. It was largely uneventful although things got lively for a while late one night when Anna, who was on watch in the cockpit, let out a scream and started dancing around in the dark. I leapt off the bunk where I had been dozing and got up top as fast as I could, heart pounding, ready for anything and wondering what could have happened to shatter the peace of the evening.

"Dad, Dad. It's a cockroach. It ran up my leg," she yelled; this from a girl who happily dived off reefs, hunted fish and swam around with sharks. I grabbed the deck broom and started looking while Anna held the torch and made suggestions. Suddenly, we spotted it lurking in amongst the main sheet tackle. It was big all right and no amount of whacking with the brush would encourage it to come out. Cockroaches may be a very primitive form of life but they it aren't daft.
I got a bucket of seawater and eventually flushed it out but it was an athlete and we lost it in the dark. A few more buckets of warm Pacific water completed the job

and we never saw it again, I could only suppose that we had managed to wash it down the cockpit drain. All the way from Scotland I had managed to avoid getting any roaches on board. Since it was in the cockpit I could only hope that it had been blown offshore ahead of one of the rain squalls we had had.

Five days after leaving Bora Bora we sailed into the harbour at Aviatu, a grubby dusty place where we moored stern on to the busy harbour wall with the anchor out ahead holding *Beyond*'s bow into the swell that rolled in through the gap in the reef. I didn't like it at all. It was expensive and provided very little shelter and all day and some part of the night huge forklifts shunted containers around on the harbour wall where the stern lines were made fast. But I didn't have to stick around long. Early one afternoon late in August Anna went ashore with her kit. We let the lines go and I hauled the boat away from the quay with the anchor, then motored out through the pass, with few regrets other than saying goodbye to my daughter.

I was happy to be on my way again and there was a reasonable forecast with fresh southerly winds for the following couple of days. As usual with a departure from the leeward side of an island, things were fairly flukey until I cleared the end of the land but when I did the wind came in strong from the south and I set the small jib and rolled away the genoa. I had a steady twenty five knots apparent on the quarter and there was a really big swell. As the afternoon wore on it was clear that there wasn't going to be much change so I settled the boat down for the night with the No 4 out to starboard, making her as comfortable as possible, although we certainly took the occasional unpredictable lurch as one of the bigger seas came up under the quarter. As it got dark it was cold enough for a jacket for the first time in months. Surely I wouldn't have to look for a pair of socks? I hadn't worn any in over six months and I wasn't sure where they were.

I hadn't been feeling good for a while. I had absolutely no appetite and little enthusiasm for life. More than ever I realised that now that Anna had left I was beginning to feel very lonely again which was a great pity and I thought rather a selfish emotion considering what I was doing, where I was, and the relative freedom I had to do whatever I wanted. It was a dismal, windy and fairly sad night and I felt angry with myself for feeling this way, sailing a beautiful boat in this wonderful ocean, when so many people in less fortunate circumstances would have given anything to be in my position.

Over the next few days the wind shifted to the northeast and *Beyond* rolled along doing just under 140 miles a day which was comfortable progress. On the third night out one of the big motor yachts we had seen in Polynesia came by and we had a chat on the VHF but, other than that, I saw nothing. A couple of very squally days followed with the wind hitting thirty knots on one occasion then things quietened down again. In general, it was easy sailing that didn't require much effort from me. I began to look forward to my arrival in Tonga, a new island group to explore and the final staging post on my long voyage to New Zealand. We crossed the dateline on the morning of August 4 and later in the afternoon I anchored off the town of Neiafu on the Island of Vavau.

13

Island Time . . .

THE bay at Neiafu is said to be one of the best hurricane holes in the Pacific. There are a few very heavy moorings for use when the cyclone season comes and plenty of other visiting boats can tie to at no great cost. Ashore, the contrast with the sophisticated and very expensive islands of Polynesia was immediately apparent. No gleaming Porches here; most of the vehicles looked as if they should have gone to the scrapyard years ago, probably as a result of running on the potholed roads with their falling in kerbs and broken drains. Shanty-style houses with pigs and chickens wandering around in the muddy yards completed the picture. But the atmosphere was cheery and laidback and with other boats I knew already there I soon settled in to day to day life in the anchorage.

It was only August and the waters just north of New Zealand would still be cold and gale swept so, of course, it would be far too early to be thinking about heading south. *Falbala* came in and so did John on the other *Beyond* and with the other boats we knew we made a happy band of wanderers. From time to time one or more of the boats would head off for a few days to explore some other bay but they always came back to the anchorage. There was Wi Fi available ashore and one day when I was looking at the World Cup site to catch up on the news I decided to email the Scottish Rugby Union to tell them about my voyage and my target of getting to New Zealand in time for the game. I was probably the supporter who had spent the longest time travelling to the event. I sent away a message and thought nothing more of it. Although we all had a good laugh at the idea, I felt in the back of my mind that I might get a T shirt or maybe even a lunch out of it.

Each Friday evening there was a very informal Cruisers Race around the bay after which everyone went ashore for beers and food. I decided to have a go, and because my old competitive spirit had not left me, I took *Beyond* round to another bay midweek and spent two days cleaning the bottom of the boat. If the other boats knew I had done it I would probably have been disqualified for cheating. Off we set on Friday, having co-opted the folk from *Falbala* and a New Zealand boat as crew. The competition was less than intense with some of the boats crossing the start line several minutes after the gun. We took the lead just after the start and held on to it to the finish, just managing to hold off a late challenge from a surprisingly fast Swiss catamaran and took first place. It was all great fun.

I modestly collected my prize and kept quiet about my clean hull.

Tonga is a very religious nation and the Sabbath is strictly observed by the people. The streets were deserted and there was a ban on any sort of recreational activity such as swimming, playing games, dancing or fishing. I got the impression that even smiling was frowned upon. On Sundays the crews of the cruising boats did what they could and kept a low profile. There was a certain rather pleasant and old world charm to it.

Tongans are well used to making do with very little and are great at getting by. It was common to see cars with missing windows, or battered doors of a different colour from the body, held shut with a bent piece of wire or a tatty piece of rope. One day a group of us set off in a mini bus to take our empty gas bottles a couple of miles down the road to the depot. The store ship had been in the day before and it was strongly rumoured that fresh stocks of gas had arrived. We juddered and bumped along the road and every so often one of the doors would fly open half way round a corner but we got used to reading the camber of the bends and anticipating the moment. At the depot we waited in line to get our bottles filled. When my turn came they didn't have an adaptor to suit my European style bottles. I was disappointed and wondered how I could get around the problem but the gas man punched a hole in a piece of thick cardboard, pushed the coupling down onto it, then sat on it to improve the seal. When he opened the valve a jet of condensed gas shot up the leg of his shorts but he didn't seem to mind and the bottle slowly filled. That was typically Tongan.

Amongst the boats in the anchorage was a very functional and fast-looking black hulled yacht with a couple and a dog on board. I had met them back in Polynesia. The owner had told me he was on his way to South Africa and hoped to get there before the end of the year. I had mentioned going to New Zealand but that course of action wasn't open to him because of the dog. He seemed to be running a bit behind and I was quite surprised to see him sitting on a mooring in Neiafu. I thought no more about it but one day when I came ashore there was clearly something amiss. Both he and his partner looked upset and the usually lively dog was lying under the table shaking and panting. It turned out that there had been an accident. Somehow the unfortunate dog had fallen over the side and become trapped under the dinghy barely avoiding drowning. Cruisers are always keen to help each other and a number of suggestions were put forward, some more sensible than others, possibly due both to an absence of knowledge about animals and to the fact that those putting them forward had embarked on happy hour some time previously. In the end the consensus was that the poor dog probably had pneumonia and that the best thing would be to give him antibiotics.

Things didn't look much better the next day and it was clear that, far from there being an improvement, the animal's condition was deteriorating. There was a vet on board one of the boats and he gave some advice but as far as I recall it was ignored. That evening another lively debate ensued whilst the poor dog lay under the table still in great distress. Incredibly, a makeshift oxygen tent was improvised from a vacuum sealed clothes storage bag and a dive bottle.

I heard no more for a while but later I noticed that the boat was not on her mooring. That evening she came back in and her owners sat alone in the bar above the dinghy dock, downcast and tearful. There was no sign of the dog and I hardly had to ask what had taken place. In a voice choked with emotion the skipper told me that Poor R was "sleeping with the fishes." Not long afterwards they sailed for New Zealand. Strangely enough the dog had been a water spaniel.

The days drifted by. I got a polite but fairly unenthusiastic acknowledgement from the SRU, which was a little disappointing, but they did ask me to let them know how I was getting on.

I began to get the paperwork sorted out for my arrival in New Zealand. Dozens of overseas yachts make the passage from the Pacific islands to New Zealand every year and Customs and Immigration in New Zealand are well used to dealing with them. They provided excellent information packs for the incoming yachts which the Internet café ashore kept in stock and the lady who ran the café was well versed in the rules. It was a good move because most mornings the place was full of yachties drinking coffee and filling in their forms. We were all looking forward to getting down there and the conversation often turned to what we would do when we got there. Although you can usually get good vegetables, other food shopping in most Pacific Islands can be a bit of a struggle. Apart from French Polynesia, where there are French style supermarkets full of hugely expensive French stuff, most of the islands have small Chinese-run stores full of really cheap tinned food, most of which is very low on quality. Now and again you would come across some tinned stuff from Australia, but it was a rarity, so it wasn't surprising that one of the things most people seemed to be looking forward to in New Zealand was access to some of the good food for which the country was renowned. I was always a bit surprised that people living on islands surrounded by seas teeming with fish should prefer to eat tinned food but they do and there are high rates of obesity and diabetes amongst the locals.

It was a very sociable time for the cruisers with more boats arriving all the time to join the crowd waiting to head south. There were film nights and rugby games shown on the screen at the bar above the dinghy dock and there always seemed to be something happening either ashore or on one of the boats.

A Scottish guy Anna and I had met back up the line in Bora Bora was skippering a Norwegian boat owned by two rather eccentric but very attractive Norwegian businesswomen. The boat's name was, believe it or not, *MAD*. He told us that that the letters were the initials of some organisation or other and now and again he would give us an insight into his life with what he referred to as The Mad Women. I think they eventually took the boat to Fiji and sold her. One evening before they left, Scott and I sat down and, over a few beers, concocted what we thought was an absolute killer email to Aurora, the essence of which was would she please let me know what she was up to and make her mind up about whether there was any future in me trying to continue our long distance relationship. I didn't want to make it sound like some sort of an ultimatum but I felt she might at least give me a clue. Sad in a way to see a 65 year old behaving like a schoolboy but it's surprising what seven months of a monastic lifestyle can do to a man. After a brief moment of self congratulation on the wording and general style of our effort we pushed the button and sent it off. At least I had done something.

Neiafu had been a lot of fun but time was going by and I needed to start heading south.

TONGA TOWARDS NEW ZEALAND

A close call and a dash south

I lay on the mooring in Vavau looking across the bay at the other yachts where my friends would be getting ready to turn in, thinking back over all the things that had happened, the places I had been and some of the wonderful people that I had met since I had so light heartedly set off from Falmouth little thinking that a year later I would be in Tonga. Now only the last leg to New Zealand remained to be sailed. I was just over 1000 miles from the North Cape, and another 100 or so from Whangerei, my target; the focus of all my efforts since leaving the Caribbean and turning west to Panama. In the larger world of ocean sailing it wasn't a great achievement. Many boats had made the same journey before but sitting in the evening calm of the anchorage at Neiafu, watching the full moon rise above the trees ashore and listening to the evening chorus of the crickets, it was special for me.

The quiet voices of cockpit conversations in other boats carried across the mirror smooth water. Further down the bay I could just make out the shape of the other *Beyond* with John and Wendy on board. They had only to reach New Zealand to have completed their long voyage around the world. I felt sure they would be feeling more or less the same way I was. Other friends from *Evangelina*, outward bound from Hawaii, rowed past in the silent twilight, their oars creaking, the shape of their little pram dinghy mirrored in the water. They called out a greeting as they passed then stopped, content to sit motionless, drifting in the moonlight. It was an evening to treasure.

I looked forward greatly to getting south and I had found myself thinking, and occasionally, talking more and more in terms of "When I get to New Zealand." I had plenty to look forward to. I would be seeing old friends again and I had the excitement of the big game to look forward to, always assuming I could get there in time. More importantly, I would have arrived somewhere that I could safely stay for six months whilst I decided what to do next. It would be a holiday and I was still hoping against hope that Aurora would accept my invitation to come over from Buenos Aires and sail with me. But she was back home after her solo Atlantic crossing, celebrating her enhanced status as an Argentinian sailing personality and feminist icon. Gloomy reports of a poor second-hand market for overseas yachts were filtering north and I began to become aware of some of the difficulties I might face if I did try to sell *Beyond* in New Zealand where she would be considered a foreign import and the proceeds of any sale would be taxed heavily. The night before I was due to head south to Nukualofa, I filled the boat with friends and we shared food and drink until late. Other sailors passing in dinghies came aboard and joined the party and it wasn't long before *Beyond* was crammed with people.

The next morning I said my final goodbyes and sailed south towards Nukualofa, the southernmost port in the Tongan group, my kicking off point for the voyage to New Zealand. I had a trouble-free light weather passage down and moored up in the harbour, with an anchor out forward and two very long stern lines tied to the harbour wall. It was the first of September and, although it was certainly very early to be setting off south, I had a month in hand and could afford to wait a few more days for suitable weather.

Vavau had had quite a bit of laid-back charm about it, but Nukualofa was very much a working port. Apart from a few banks and a couple of coffee shops in town, most of the town was run down and dirty with badly made and potholed roads. The two smartest buildings in the place were the Chinese Embassy and the King's Palace and there was no escaping the fact that, as in so many other islands in the Western Pacific, the Chinese influence was gradually taking over. There were dozens of roadside stalls, all selling the same selection of vegetables and a big open-air market area with covered stalls, all selling the same range of stuff, most of it cheaply made and imported. The people here clearly had just as little as the folk in the north, the only difference was that they lived in a town, with more paved roads and fewer pigs and dogs wandering around. I wasn't tempted to stay any longer than I had to but there was no point in setting off on a bad forecast and the later I left the more the New Zealand Spring should have taken hold and the less the chances were of running into bad weather as I got further south.

After ten days I had had enough and decided to set off. There wasn't much wind forecast but time was wearing on and I wanted to get on my way. So I cleared Customs, motored out though the reef and headed off towards the south. There was even less wind than the forecast had promised and after 40 hours of creeping along, and some spells of motoring, I gave it up as a bad job and turned back. I should have gone into the harbour and reported in but I sailed over to Pangiamoto Island instead and anchored off the reef hoping to get away again within a day or so. That turned out to be a big mistake. The next morning the weather turned unsettled and I put out a second anchor but within a matter of hours a roll of cloud came along and a fearsome squall came through. The wind quickly increased from ten to thirty knots then up to thirty five and shifted about forty degrees, with driving rain. The rain was so heavy that I couldn't see the shore only 50 yards away and the wind was so strong that I couldn't hear the engine. I was working blind. To make things worse the wind shift meant that I was no longer in the shelter off the reef and I started to drag towards it. I had no choice but to get out, which I only just managed, losing my second anchor in the process before scuttling back into the harbour. I had avoided going onto the reef and I was angry at the loss of the anchor but my troubles had only just begun. Back inside the main port I had no choice but to report to Customs, who wanted to know why I had come back and when I had arrived? There was no point in being smart and when I told them where I had been and for how long they became very angry, indeed, because I had not immediately reported my arrival but had, in their words, "hidden" in Pangiamoto, as an illegal entrant to the country which was technically true. There was no doubt about it. They were mightily angry. I was lucky to escape a heavy fine and was ordered to report to their office every morning at nine to advise them of my plans to depart.

But Tonga had one more bit of excitement in store which very nearly put an end to my progress for a while.

The World Cup games were being shown on a big screen in the 'Billfish Bar' on the road that ran along the shore side of the harbour. On the night of the Tonga v Canada match I wandered over to watch the game. As soon as I got in it was clear that World Cup fever had taken charge and the joint was jumping. There was a country band playing, Tongan flags were everywhere, the booze was flowing and the crowd were getting pumped up and ready to go to war. I happily joined in assuming temporary Tongan loyalties.

But Tonga lost and the mood moved from buoyant anticipation to rowdy disappointment. The crowd changed as well with some of the diehard rugby fans heading off and the usual late night crowd coming in. Up at the bar I was trying to hear the post-match discussion on the TV but the evening was no longer about sport and the sound had been turned down. To delay my return to the boat for yet another solitary night, I had stayed on for a couple of final cleansing ales, but *Beyond* was at anchor and with a dinghy ride across the dark and windy harbour ahead of me,w it was time to call it a night and head home. Then one of the bar girls handed me cold bottle of beer and gestured towards a table of Tongan ladies who were clearly out to party, and where one, in what had once been a fairly smart backless cocktail dress, waved hello.

What should I do now? I could hardly send the beer back and, with my natural shyness subdued by drink, the choice between an early return to an empty boat and joining a table of partying ladies was easy so I wandered over to the table. But that was just the start of it. For whatever reason my backless chum had clearly decided that I was target for tonight and even though the music was so loud that conversation was almost impossible, it was clear that I was in for more than a cultural exchange. Well, it was party night. Things were going fine until a very large guy in a Tongan shirt joined the table and started to give me hard time. "Who are you, man?", he said. I introduced myself and he shook my hand in a grip that could have crushed a brick, but would not let go. Oops, things were taking an unfortunate turn. I could see trouble coming and I realised that I was the only European in the place. I wasn't sober but this guy was worse and clearly angry both about the result and the fact that I seemed to be horning in on the local night life, even if it had been by invitation. "You like Tongan pussy, man? You want f*** Tongan pussy?", he said. It wasn't exactly small talk. He could have killed me with one hand.

Backless managed to calm things down a bit but getting whacked by some huge Tongan for sitting with the wrong girl had no appeal. Even in my over refreshed condition I realised that and I had to get out. I mumbled something about too much beer and made tracks for the gents out at the back then nipped round the end of the building and onto the road just as Backless appeared out of the front door, closely followed by Man Mountain both looking for me but for different reasons. Now I may not be much of a fighter but I can run. I set off along the dark road at top speed and I was going well until one of my flip fops came off and I went down on my knees in the grit. I got up fast but there was no need. I was obviously not worth chasing. My hands were grazed and my foot hurt. I limped the rest of the way back to the dinghy and rowed out to the *Beyond.*

The next morning I looked back at the previous night's carry on and realised I had been lucky. I had a thick head, a broken toe and only one flip flop but I was alive.

What with that and my earlier narrow escape from dragging onto the reef, I was beginning to think that perhaps Nukualofa was not the place for me and finally on September 17 with 13 days to go to the game and time running out, I presented my outward clearance papers and set off, under strict instructions not to return. I assured them that I would do my best and slunk off like a bad schoolboy.

I motored out round the island and towards the gap in the reef in mirror calm conditions. I had as much fuel on board as I could possibly carry and more than enough food and water. As far as the weather was concerned I would have to take my chances because I had clearly outstayed my welcome and, anyway, I couldn't hang around any longer if I wanted to be in Auckland in time to get to the match. The Scottish Rugby Union had, so far, seemed unimpressed with my efforts but we were still in touch and they were starting to sound a little more interested so I sent another email telling them I had left and was on my way. Mind you, I had told them that once already, so I wasn't surprised when they just replied: 'Let us know how you get on'. I sailed in a light southerly breeze all night but by noon the next day I had more wind than I needed and was down to my usual windy weather rig of two reefs and the number four. To start with the wind was right ahead but it gradually shifted and I made good progress along the track for just over a day before it died again and I resorted to using the engine for a while. I certainly couldn't just sit there and the further south we got the more likelihood there was that we would get a steady breeze which continued to come and go.

Finally, on the afternoon of the fifth day things began to settle down a little. Mid-way through the afternoon we passed from west into east Longitude, confirming that, geometrically, at least, I had sailed half-way around the world. I had hoped to film the change as it was came up on the GPS screen but I got distracted and missed the event so I had to make do with showing the new figures. We had passed out of the tropics the previous day and there was a definite drop in temperature. I had been wearing a fleece in the evenings for a while and on the same day as we crossed the 180th meridian I pulled a rather musty pair of long trousers out from the locker and put them on. It was the first time I had worn anything other than shorts in ten months.

Around twenty seven degrees south a succession of cold fronts came through with lots of wind and heavy rain and, for a while, I sailed in fast and wet conditions, hard on the wind on the port tack. It began to look as if I wasn't going to weather the North Cape and I really had no wish to get anywhere to the west of it in this unsettled Spring weather. I was at least month too early in heading south from Tonga and I knew from my years at sea how bad things could be off the North Cape if I got caught in a gale. In the winter of 1967, in one of the worst nights I had ever experienced at sea, we had tried to help a New Zealand ship which had run aground on the bank but she was lost with all hands and we saw nothing but wreckage. Things were so bad that a couple of life buoys from our ship had been washed into the sea. The shore search party found them washed up on Ninety Mile beach and for a while it was feared that our vessel had been lost as well.

So I was very glad when the wind began to back and we started to get lifted towards the east. Three hundred miles out things began to look optimistic. It was windy and cold and the nights were dark but I was making good progress. Not wanting to close the coast until I was almost as far south as Bream Head, I kept as far off as I could and on the evening of September 27 I knew that I was looking at the final sunset of the long voyage from Scotland and that I was in striking distance of my destination. The following morning the sun rose to give me my first sight of the Northland coast. I drank my tea and looked at the beautiful shades of green on the hills on shore as beyond sailed surely on. I had just over 30 miles to go. It was almost over.

I had been hard on the wind on the same tack for days, but the wind was dying and I wasn't going to get round Bream Head at the entrance to Whangerei on that tack. Having come so far I couldn't bring myself to start the engine so a mile north of the island I made one 500 yard tack out to the east to clear the magnificently towering Bream Head and bore away towards the channel entrance. By late afternoon I was tied up on the quarantine berth at Marsden Cove handing over my forms and doing my customs inspection and by six in the evening I was alone on the boat again.

A short tack to clear Bream Head

I sat in the cockpit and let my thoughts crowd in. Despite the dire warnings from other cruisers I had managed to get down from Tonga by the end of September. I had a six month visa, a ticket to see the game in Auckland and the long New Zealand summer stretching ahead of me. A huge sense of relief swept over me. It had been a long haul from Scotland but I had made it.

14

Off to the Game

Scotland the Brave

EARLY next morning on my way up the channel towards the town basin I got a call from the Scottish Rugby Union congratulating me on my voyage from Scotland and asking if I would like to come down to Auckland and meet up with them. I could hardly believe it as the game was only two days away and they wanted to use the story of *Beyond*'s voyage as part of their pre-match build up. But hang on I hadn't even told my friend Helen in Auckland that I had arrived and, though I knew Auckland was not far away, I only had the vaguest idea of how to get there. Maybe there was a bus I could catch.

"Can you get up to Whangarei airport by seven tomorrow morning?"

"Yes, sure." But how do I tell them I can only afford the bus?

"There's a ticket waiting for you at the check-in. Just get on the plane and leave it to us."

I almost ran the boat up the shore as I simply couldn't believe it. I was off to the game in a style I had never imagined possible. But first I had to get *Beyond* safely tied alongside in the basin which, thankfully, turned out to be fairly simple because I really couldn't concentrate on what to do next. A shower would be a good idea and I had better find some decent clothes.

The rest of the day passed in a daze and early the next morning I landed at Auckland where I was met by the Public Relations team from the SRU and whisked off to the hotel where they and the team were staying. In the space of a few hours I had moved from the spartan surroundings of my boat to the spotless opulence of one of the best hotels in Auckland. It was hard to take it in. Would I like something to eat? I certainly would. I had been so worried about missing the plane earlier in the morning that I hadn't slept much and had only managed a cup of coffee before leaving the boat. My benefactors laughed as, like a man just out of jail, I tucked into the biggest New Zealand-style breakfast the hotel could provide. Would I mind doing a short radio interview? How could I say no? So we did it right there at the table.

I was beginning to think that this was a dream after all. There I was talking face to face with some of the great men I had watched over the years. Men who, in their time, had been amongst the best players in the world and they were talking to me as if I was the one who had done something worthwhile. It didn't seem quite right somehow.

Helen arrived with the now famous ticket and it was great to see her again.

After lunch Al Kellock, the Scottish Captain, made time to come down to the harbour and we did some more interviews and a bit of television. I was starting to enjoy my new lifestyle, but by the early evening all the unaccustomed activity and excitement had begun to take their toll. I hadn't had a decent night's sleep in days and although I was invited to go out again in the evening, I just couldn't make it. I was completely whacked and by early evening I was sound asleep in the most comfortable surroundings I had been in for a very long time. The next day I floated around Auckland in a relaxed state of well fed and well rested contentment, enjoying the atmosphere around the harbour and sharing a few beers with the hundreds of kilted and noisy fans who had come over from Scotland by more conventional means. In the evening Helen and I walked out to Eden Park and watched while Scotland narrowly missed beating the Auld Enemy. Life is not a succession of happy endings and it was a long walk back to town but I had had a wonderful time.

Two days later I was back in Whangarei on my boat, with its well-worn and basic interior, narrow bunks and little cooker. I knew how Cinderella must have felt after the ball. I had enjoyed a brief glimpse of another world and I would never forget the kindness and friendly company of the people who had made it all possible.

The Town Basin in Whangarei is a wonderful place and every year dozens of cruising boats from all over the world find their way down there to lay-up while they dodge the Pacific cyclone season, rest, re-fit and replenish their stores. There is a very strong infrastructure of marine-related businesses around the harbour, some of which are run by cruisers who came years ago to visit and stayed to settle and others whose local ownership goes back for generations. These are very practical and helpful people, as well as being very welcoming and there is pretty much nothing large or small that can't be done. The annual invasion of visiting yachts brings in a vast amount of work to the marine community and, of course, a lot of income to the town as sailors, Many of them have spent a year or more up in the islands enjoy the benefits of being back where everything they need is readily available. It's a win win situation if ever there was one.

The town realises this and extends a warm welcome to the sailors who, for their part, can relax in a location where their boats are completely secure and they are amongst the sailing friends they have made further up the line. So I settled in and made myself at home. The boat came out for her refit and I took the chance to do some of the long outstanding jobs that I hadn't been able to tackle when she was afloat. While the boat was in the yard I finally got word from Aurora that she would come over to New Zealand in April and sail with me up to Fiji. Well, that was certainly something to think about.

I had bought an audio course in Spanish conversation in a moment of optimism several months ago and I started listening with renewed enthusiasm, walking around town with the I-Pod in my pocket and my earphones on, joining in with the lesson and talking to myself in Spanish. Other pedestrians must have wondered whether I had become demented as a result of long hours alone at sea.

Jim and Linda Powers whom I had met up in Ahe arrived on *Chesapeake* and we enjoyed many convivial evenings on one boat or the other and spent Christmas day picnicking on the beach. Happy days indeed.

My friends came up from Auckland and I was able to catch up with Paul, local sailing legend, now back on his home turf after his season in Polynesia. It was a great time and I made the most of it. With the boat back in the water and looking good we cruised around eating and drinking well and enjoying life to the full. Richard, an old friend from Scotland, came out for a couple of weeks and we sailed up north and then out to Barrier Island. It was great fun. Richard and I had been sailing together and getting into mischief of one sort of another back in Scotland for over 35 years and he already knew Helen so it all tuned into a big re-union and we sailed back in to Auckland and had a party on board in Westhaven, the huge marina a short walk from the centre of town. I wandered around the harbour looking at some of the magnificent super yachts, rode the ferries and, generally, did my best to look like a local. I was in a wonderful country amongst real friends and in a couple of months I would be heading for Fiji with Aurora. I may have been pretty hard up after the re-fit but I didn't have much to complain about.

One weekend I sheltered in a cove over on Barrier Island while what the locals call 'a weather bomb' went through. To qualify as a bomb the central pressure in the system has to drop by a certain amount in a certain time which provides some pretty spectacular conditions. This one certainly lived up to its name and, although I should have been well enough sheltered in the cove, the wind howling over the hills ashore dumped vertically down on to the water with gusts coming from all sorts of crazy angles. I had lots of chain down but I sheered about in the pitch dark all night, often heeling well over with the force of the wind, sitting in the cockpit drinking tea and watching the anchor lights of the boats round about in case *Beyond* should drag but she held fast. The good thing about these systems is that they go through quickly and by early the following afternoon things had settled down sufficiently to let me get some sleep. Just as well. I had been up for 30 hours and I was ready for a rest.

The east coast of the North Island has some of the best cruising areas and some of the most beautiful anchorages in the world and I did my best to get to know them. In particular the Bay of Islands is magnificent and anchoring there is a piece of cake compared to the reefs of the Pacific Islands or the kelp strewn and rocky bottomed sea lochs of Scotland. The bay also has some wonderful little ports, like Paihia and Russell, home to the George Hotel, the oldest licensed premises in New Zealand and still one of the most pleasant.

As a town Russell has a great reputation going back to the late 17th and 18th centuries when, as a base for the sailing whalers, it was known as the "Hell Hole of the Pacific". The ships would spend up to a year hunting whales in the Pacific then come down to Russell to re-fit and give the boys a much-needed run ashore. The town grew around this and it soon became a wonderful lawless mix of boatyards, bars and brothels. Local ladies would move aboard and keep the boys company for the re-fit season in return for which they would end up with a baby for themselves and a bag of nails or possibly a gun for their fathers ashore. Everyone was doing nicely until the missionaries arrived and declared the whole thing an abomination. The locals began to see the light, got themselves baptised and gave it all up; as a result of which the town descended into economic gloom. These days its colourful past is the cornerstone of its very successful tourist industry and the place has a lovely easy going air about it.

As the day of Aurora's arrival got closer I began to get nervous and I couldn't help wonder if we would be able to recapture the easy going and close relationship we had enjoyed in the Caribbean a year previously. Quite a lot had happened since. She had successfully sailed alone through some pretty dreadful weather and got her boat and herself safely to the Portugal. I had come over 6000 miles in *Beyond* there would be plenty to talk about.

I had booked a room in a hotel by the harbour and on the big day I drove down to Auckland to meet the flight. It was fine and she looked great for someone just off a long international flight. It turned out that her high profile in Argentina had worked in her favour and she had been upgraded to First Class and had spent most of the flight sipping champagne. In fact it didn't take us long to get back to where we had left off or for Aurora to come down to earth and the familiar realities of life on a sailing boat. We stayed in Whangarei for a while then set off to explore the wonderful places I now knew so well.

By mid-April we were up in Opua and ready to head north. There were a lot of boats assembling to join a rally also bound for Fiji and we were anxious to set off and stay ahead of them.

15

Fiji

Reefs, Roots and Islands

YACHTS going north from New Zealand in the spring leave on the back of a low pressure system which gives following winds to push them up clear of the coast and on towards the trade wind zone. So after hanging around for a couple of weeks waiting for the right weather we cleared outwards and headed off. But 50 miles out in the middle of the night we were close to reaching under two reefs and the staysail in a big sea in the pitch dark when there was a spectacular bang and the boat shook as if she had been hit by a hammer. The windward lower shroud had parted company with the deck. Chaos. I had a boom guy on and couldn't tack immediately so I had to cut it fast to get round onto the other tack. To add to the difficulties my Spanish deserted me in the heat of the moment and all I could think of to say was 'Donde estan los servicios?' Where are the toilets? Which looking back was probably quite appropriate. But Aurora quickly realised what had happened and, after a tense few minutes, we were able to head back towards the coast. I went up on deck to secure the loose shroud and saw that the failure had been at the toggle at the bottom of the bottle screw, something I had never seen happen before. Thankfully, we were able to get back into Opua without having to tack. If the wind had shifted the other way we would have had to run up the coast to the north and God knows where we would have wound up. But it worked out and after clearing inwards again we moored in the marina and I replaced the toggles and lower bottle screw sections on all the shrouds. After a full rig check, another few days of waiting and more customs formalities, we set off again.

The trip north was tough with some of the most unpleasant sailing conditions I had experienced since leaving the UK. We got the promised following weather for the first two days but it then came ahead and we spent a couple of days heading into it double reefed with the staysail in very rough seas and a big confused swell. I was glad to have had the rig checked. Thankfully, it wasn't cold because we certainly got wet. The wind gradually came round onto the quarter again and after a short lull began to really blow. Coupled with a big swell and two wave systems running across each other it made life on board miserable.

With the boat unable to get into any sort of rhythm, cooking and eating were a chore and it was a struggle to simply hang on. Aurora is quite a bit shorter than I am so I had put two new grab handles up on the deckhead which made hanging on easier especially when coming down through the hatch.Aurora knew as well as anyone how important it was to hang on tight in that sort of weather but, even so, five days out, she was thrown across the boat and landed heavily on her lower spine on the galley crash bar. The situation was made worse by the

151

fact that I followed and landed on top of her. I got up but she was stunned and sat there too worried about her spine to try and move. I was seriously concerned as well so I strapped a board to the small of her back with a couple of sail ties and, as gently as I could under the conditions, I got her immobilised in the port bunk, jammed between the lee cloth and the table, padded as much as possible with cushions. She could move her feet and wiggle her toes so things didn't look too bad but it would be a couple of days before we could rule out any internal problems. We got through to an Argentinean doctor friend on the Sat phone and were pleased when he re assured us that we had done the right thing and that the very strong painkillers the pharmacist back home had given me were just what was required.

After a couple of anxious days it was clear that everything internal was functioning properly but the weather was still bad and I was now in the position of having to sail the boat, look after myself and get enough sleep, whilst nursing and feeding an increasingly grumpy Argentinean. But I suppose it's hard to stay cheerful confined to your bunk with a bread board strapped to your back. The bad weather continued and one night I came below late, tired and wet after changing a sail. I badly wanted to sleep but I managed to cook some food for us both. Diplomatic relations became strained to say the least when my patient complained that there wasn't enough olive oil on the potatoes. Things gradually got easier and I was able to set the main deep-reefed and start making real progress and Aurora was able first to sit up and then move cautiously around the boat. We were both very glad when, after nine days at sea, we got through the reef and into the shelter of the bay at Savu Savu on Vanua Levu, the northernmost of the two main Fiji Islands. It was pitch dark and our chart had no detail of the creek past the headland but we motored very slowly upstream between the dark silhouettes of the moored boats until the echo sounder warned us to go no further.

The next day we tried to get on to one of the vacant moorings at the Copra Shed, with its smart little sailing club and bar, but I was told that they were all reserved for the Rally boats expected any day from New Zealand so we went further down the creek and the social scale to Wai Tui Marina where we were warmly welcomed and helped onto the mooring by their boatman. Wai Tui was not so much a marina as a collection of semi-submerged mooring buoys off the end of a very rickety jetty with two grubby toilets and a club which consisted of a couple of wooden tables and an ancient and rusty fridge full of frosty bottles of cold beer. Whatever it might have lacked in terms of sophistication it more than made up for in the warmth of its welcome. The whole place had a wonderful air to it and many boats had been on the buoys for months. We were handed a sheet of paper containing the marina rules which pretty much summed up the laid back atmosphere.

> *Try not to get drunk and fall in the Dock.*
> *If you fall in the Dock, try and float face up.*
> *Smile and Laugh a lot.*

After a couple of weeks, during which we rested and did a little exploring, Aurora left to head back to her own boat which was still in Portugal, and solo once again, I set off with the aim of sailing around the main island of Vanua Levu.

Sailing around the coast of Fiji is not easy for a number of reasons as there are very few large scale charts. Many areas have never been surveyed or were surveyed long ago. In some cases the information is attributed to Cook and Bligh! More than half of the beacons on the reefs are missing and those that are there are usually about the size of a broom handle. The general detail of the surveys is very poor. Many areas are just left blank.

It's not possible to transfer GPS positions straight on to the Admiralty charts without adjusting them and whilst you can do so on the Fijian Charts, these bear the rather disturbing information that 'WGS 84 positions can be plotted directly onto this chart, however, they will be more accurate than the charted position of the land.'

So where does that leave you? Confused, in my case.

In addition, you can forget the plotter in most areas. Although you may have the right chip it is impossible to zoom in because you are simply left with a load of dots instead of detail. Even when you can zoom in the graphic display of where you are supposed to be is simply wrong - often by as much as a quarter of a mile or more. I crept through a pass in the reef and into a bay one evening trying to get some shelter in the lee of a low island. Watching the echo sounder constantly, I dropped the hook in about seven metres and went below where the plotter showed me to be in amongst the palm trees about half a mile inshore. It soon became clear that the only things I could rely on were my eyes and the echo sounder. All of this makes life a little difficult since even an agile solo sailor cannot be up looking for coral heads and in the cockpit steering at the same time.

Resting At Wai Tui

It also pays to watch the weather very carefully particularly in the early part of the summer season. The weather in Fiji depends not so much on pressure as on temperature and humidity, with the position of the convergence zone to the north playing a major part, either giving days of blue skies and fine weather or days of low cloud and very strong winds. The barometer isn't really much help and the best clue is often just to watch the clouds. After a few weeks you get a feel for it.

As far as the sea goes there is very little between the Fiji islands and the South American continent except water and when it's been blowing from the southeast for a few days, as it often does, there is a very big sea and swell running which shortens and gets very steep as it reaches the reefs. Because the great majority of the reefs are just below the surface, and invisible in settled weather, getting in and out of the poorly charted and unmarked passes can be a tense experience. In many ways it's easier when it's rough because the sea breaks on the reef and you can see where the gap is.

The first day of my cruise round Vanua Levu was eventful to say the least. Leaving Savu Savu I headed out of the pass through the reef and with about 30 miles to go to the next pass, I began to reach along the coast in a fresh southerly which picked up and drew ahead as the cloud base lowered to windward. After a couple of hours by which time I was double reefed, I picked up a Mayday from a New Zealand couple whose boat had hit the coral coming out of one of the passes through the reef. They were taking a lot of water and trying to get to the next pass a few miles to the west and the position they gave was just a few miles to leeward of mine. I told them I would be there in about 30 minutes, and headed back downwind and inshore, hoping to be able to float some gear down to them and get them off. After about five minutes they came up on VHF again, saying they were now fast aground on the reef and pounding badly in the swell. To make matters worse they had become separated with the skipper still on the boat and his wife who had the radio in the raft. It was dreadful to hear the desperation in her voice and to realise that because they were on the reef I could nothing to help. I arrived after about 20 minutes by which time it was blowing hard, with very steep seas and swell rebounding from the reef. Their boat was on its side with the half unfurled genoa roaring and flapping in the wind, and she was being pounded against the reef by the waves. Beyond the boat I could see the orange canopy of the raft, which

The boat was on its side on the reef

seemed to have been washed over the reef. In these conditions I was seriously worried about my own position. I sailed *Beyond* up and down a hundred yards to weather under deep reefed main only, relaying messages and keeping the raft in sight. After about an hour to my immense relief I was told that a local boat had come out from the lee side of the reef and that they were both okay but I had a very tough beat to get off to weather and round to the next pass to the east, finally getting through and anchoring just before darkness fell.

The next day the two Kiwis very kindly came by in a motor boat to say thanks and I felt a real sense of satisfaction at having been able to help, even in a small way. They said it had been great to know that I was watching and relaying all the facts to the boats anchored a few miles away. Their yacht had broken up during the night and they had been unable to retrieve much. I tried to reassure them and said: "Don't worry, you will be sailing again," to which the lady replied: "Well he might, I bloody won't."

After a couple of days resting I carried on to the north , first to Katharine Bay then to a beautiful anchorage in the lagoon at Albert Cove where I stayed for a few days taking it easy, swimming and socialising with the other two boats there, an American and a Dane. The cove is deserted apart from two huts set back amongst the palms, where a total of three people lived, eeking out a meagre existence from copra. The rowdy weather passed and I enjoyed a wonderful open water sail in fabulous blue green seas and flashing white crests across to the north tip of Vanua Levu and down the other side and entering the pass through the Great Sea Reef and finding a sheltered anchorage. The remainder of my trip round the island was done inside the reef, with a great deal of care, and hundreds of visual hand bearing compass fixes. Every day I searched for missing beacons and unmarked passages through between the inner reefs.

I came to the last anchorage of the cruise in the evening of my thirteenth day out and quietly congratulated myself on having it made it in one piece. But there's many a slip. The weather came in again in the morning and leaving the anchorage in flat grey light and poor visibility, I hit the same coral outcrop I had managed to avoid on the way in. I was going slowly but I was badly shaken and the rest of the trip back was rather spoilt.

Back in Savu Savu I spent a few days anchored up the creek then set off again over to Viti Levu to explore that island. I can tell you that I was being very careful. The open water trip over is about 30 miles and I had glorious conditions with a beam wind. Being on the leeward side of the island I had flattish water. It was a great trip and I found the pass in through the main reef of Viti Levu and re-entered the sheltered water early in the evening. Over the next week I sailed slowly round the northwestern part of Viti Levu past Lautoka, and down into the marina at Vuda Point where you lie bow on to the circular quay with stern lines to buoys. Most importantly, they have a travel lift and I was able to haul out and have the boat surveyed. I had already established that there was no sign of damage, internally, as a result of my contact with the reef but nonetheless I was greatly relieved when she came clear of the water and we saw nothing more than some scraped paint. I wiped her down and launched again. *Beyond* is a tough boat. I slept well that night, I can tell you.

Fijians are naturally cheerful and friendly people who love to sing and drink beer or the more traditional Fijian brew, kava, made from the kava root which, in the past, was chewed by the village virgins until it was soft and then made into a drink. These days, possibly due to a shortage of virgins or perhaps a higher general regard for hygiene, its pounded mechanically. When added to water it makes a drink which looks and tastes like runny wallpaper paste. Kava drinking is very much a man thing. The guys sit around a big bowl of the stuff from which they fill a smaller bowl. They pass the small bowl round each man draining it in one go amongst much chat, hand clapping and general goodwill. After a while they either fall asleep or look for a fight, just like home really. I tried it on a couple of occasions and found it turned my face numb but for safety's sake I stuck to a single bowl then left. No more Tongan style escapes for me, thank you.

Vuda Point is a great spot but I really wanted to get out to the Yasawas, a chain of islands running north and south out to the west but I was nervous. I had seen enough of the reefs and islands to realise that sailing solo was simply too risky. One grounding was enough and knowing how misleading the GPS was, it was obvious that if I was going to able to visit the islands without making any further contact with the coral I would need to get someone else on board to be up on the bow looking for problems as we tried to get through the passes to anchor in the lagoons. It was no good relying on the echo sounder either because the coral heads rise almost vertically from the bottom and, by the time the echo sounder tells you it's getting shallow, it's too late to stop no matter how slowly you had been going.

So, taking my courage in both hands, I did something I had resisted doing since leaving home and contacted one of the many people advertising around the marina as crew. At Vuda Point the laundry was the place to hear all the gossip and look at the hand-written crew ads pinned to the wall. I looked over a few and got into contact with a lady who was looking for a place on a boat. The next day she arrived on board and we sat in the cockpit while I explained why, despite having sailed all the way from Scotland, I now wanted a crew. I think she believed me but, just in case, she made it very clear that she had no interest in any sort of relationship other than that of skipper and crew and that she wanted to learn as much as possible about handling the boat and navigation. It was understandable as there were plenty of tales of female crew signing on a new boat and spending all their time trying to stay out of the skipper's clutches. So I assured her that she could have the aft cabin to herself and that I wouldn't enter, unless perhaps if it was on fire, and only then after knocking. We also agreed to split feeding costs and, finally, we agreed that she would take responsibility for us not starving, I would take responsibility for us not drowning and teach her as much as she could absorb which turned out to be a lot.

The arrangement worked very well. Linda turned out to be a terrific cook and very amusing company. She had spent many years with a successful session musician in Nashville and had a fund of stories most of which seemed to centre on parties. She had also embraced

Buddhism, which made little practical difference to day to day life on board, although she would say a short prayer to any bug that was squashed. One day, hearing a strange noise, I went up into the cockpit and found her talking to the fish. After a few days we were getting on splendidly so we sailed over to Musket Cove where we stayed for a few days joining in the general social life with other cruisers and getting the boat ready for the trip north. She told me it was a new experience to be on a boat where everything worked and where she felt secure.

The weather was terrific with lots of sunshine and good sailing breezes during the day and quiet evenings. We explored the Yasawa Islands, swimming, visiting small fishing villages and anchoring in a different bay or lagoon every evening, enjoying a drink and a good dinner then retiring to our separate ends of the boat.

In these small islands the villages are usually set back from the beach behind a few palm trees and they are very peaceful places. It would have been entirely wrong to just wander around without asking permission and the usual thing was to revert to the ancient custom of presenting Sevu Sevu to the chief. The villagers, of course, had already seen the boat coming into the bay and were expecting a visit and they took us along to the chief's hut. He then summoned a few of his right hand men and the visitors and elders sit opposite each other on the floor of the hut.

Navadra, Yasawa Islands

The visitor places a bunch of Kava root on the sand in front of the chief and explains that they have sailed for many miles to visit the village and would like his permission to stay for a few days. The chief then delivers a short speech in Fijian with much hand clapping and, if he is prepared to extend a welcome, he picks up the kava and accepts the gift. He is also offering his protection whilst you are in the village. The only problem being that in return, if he decides to go off to war with another island whilst you are there, you are obliged to pick up your club and fall in behind him. Thankfully, we arrived at a time of peace and stability. The villagers lead a very simple life, which seems to revolve around the church and the school. The dwellings were basic. Most of the cooking was being done on wood burning stoves. Fijians are very loyal and, since many young men left from these villages to fight in the Second World War, most of the villages have a small war memorial.

Pigs and dogs are communal property and wander around at will and usually a pig will be slaughtered on some special occasion. The people travel between the small islands in big fibreglass longboats with powerful outboards. In the mornings boatloads of school children and adults would come by waving hello on their way off to wherever they were going for the day. Other boats with young Fijian guys on board would also come by on their way to fish and dive on the reef. Some of these used to anchor quite close in the evenings but that might have been because Linda liked to enjoy her morning tea on deck in her bikini. Fishermen go away out beyond the reef in fragile canoes some of which are made by simply folding a corrugated iron sheet in half, putting a thwart in the middle and nailing the ends together. On the passage you would come across these guys, well over a mile out from their village, paddling and patiently fishing with nylon lines and hooks. One day we stopped the boat close by one of these canoes and I gave the fisherman a box of hooks and weights I had bought in New Zealand and never used. You would think he had won the lottery. I felt very humble. Before long it was time to head back to Musket Cove for a few days of comparative luxury lying on a mooring. We visited the shore to take showers, did some laundry and joined in the evening happy hour with other sailors at the little bar on the sand spit. Then we headed back across to Vuda Point where Linda, now much more confident than when we had set off, took *Beyond* up the narrow channel through the reef past the bar and the restaurant crowded with the sunset customers. I stood below, out of sight in the hatch, ready to take over if anything went wrong but nothing did. I think that was probably one of the highlights of her trip. On my part it had been great to have someone else on board who had been so eager to learn and was such good company.

It is impossible to describe fully the whole Fiji experience ashore and afloat in just a few pages. The abiding memories are of wide blue skies, beautiful beaches and smiling people. I think it is a wonderful place, not without its own economic problems, but with a population who's friendly and helpful attitude make every day a pleasure. The food is good, much of the scenery, particularly in the outer islands, is stunningly beautiful and even in the towns one feels completely safe, and welcome. It may have been a struggle getting there but it had been very much worth it.

Sadly, you can't slow down the seasons and I wanted to get back down south to New Zealand for the coming summer. I had to take the boat round to Lautoka to complete clearance formalities. Once you have your clearance you are required to go to sea immediately and clear territorial waters as fast as you can. I didn't want another Tongan-style episode so even though the pass through the reef was miles away and well out of sight of the harbour I headed straight out.

For three days the wind blew hard from the southeast and I spent a lot of time under much reduced sail listening to forecasts and watching the barometer. I was getting pushed too far to the west, just where I didn't want to be, with a low pressure system starting to approach. On the fourth day the wind shifted further into the north then into northwest and stayed there for a few days which let me get back to the east a bit. The seas were pretty big and, on the afternoon of the seventh day, the lashing holding the turning block for the monitor lines parted and the boat broached. I was pretty busy for a while getting things back under control but it was an easy thing to fix and we were soon off again.

Twenty four hours out from Opua the wind came ahead again and I had a very windy and cold beat in an uncomfortable sea before I finally got in and tied up on the quarantine berth. But I was in and, once again, the New Zealand summer with all that it promised stretched ahead. A few days later sailed I down to Bream Head and then up the river with the tide to the Town Basin where Sharon from the marina took my lines and gave me a hug.

Welcome home. That was exactly how it felt.

16

The Dark Islands

Farewell to New Zealand

BEYOND had spent the cyclone season in New Zealand based in Town Basin Whangarei along with many other cruising yachts. I had used Whangarei as my home port during both my seasons in New Zealand and had got to know other members of the cruising community well, along with many of the locals in the marine industry. There are always interesting boats and people there nearly all of whom have come just as long a distance as I had and some of whom I had first met further up the line in Polynesia, Tonga and Fiji over the past two years. We made quite a little village and being part of the cruising community was a real pleasure. I spent some weeks moored astern of *Nina,* an American schooner, built in 1928 and one of the most successful yachts in American racing history. She was also the first-ever American yacht to win the Fastnet race. She was still very much in her original form and down below the dates of her most famous race wins were carved into her deck beams. I got to know Rosemary and her son, David, well. I had embarked on the mammoth task of recaulking *Beyond*'s teak decks and I spent five weeks on my knees gouging, drilling, sanding and caulking. It was a good idea when I started but it quickly turned into a form of daily torture.

Other sailors walking past would shake their heads and offer encouragement and passing locals and tourists would lean over the rail on the edge of the quay and joke about the job I was making of it. I almost became one of the curiosities of the harbour.

I wanted to get away up the coast as soon as possible after Christmas but the tides were wrong for getting down the river so just before the big day I left Town Basin and moved down to Marsden Point, a modern but completely soulless marina development at the mouth of the estuary. A weather system moved in and it blew hard and rained for a few days. Everything was closed up ashore and I think there was only one other boat there with anyone on board. It was hardly a festive occasion but two days before Christmas came the wonderful news of the birth of my first grandchild, a beautiful girl called Isla, three weeks early but perfect in every way. I opened the champagne I had been saving for the occasion and remembered the way I had felt the night my son had been born. Things had gone full circle and I could well imagine how Robert and Susanna must be feeling right now. Forget sailing half way round the world, nothing compares with looking at your own new-born child. It would be almost two years before I would finally meet her but the thought of her new life and of my new role as a grandfather filled me with a great feeling of warmth and belonging even though I was thousands of miles away.

During that New Zealand summer, which was the driest and hottest for years, I cruised between Auckland and the North Cape. I grew to love the magnificent Northland coast with its many beautiful bays and secure anchorages. It is a wonderful part of the world and it would take pages and pages of description and scores of photographs to do it justice. Better still, Aurora came over from Buenos Aires and we cruised together for a few weeks enjoying many quiet evenings at anchor in some of our favourite bays and re-visiting the places we had enjoyed so much the previous year before our trip north to Fiji. We were both used to being completely independent and sailing our own boats in our own way and spending months apart on opposite sides of the world just seemed to make the reunions more pleasurable. We spent some time up in the beautiful harbour at Whangaroa, anchored beneath the towering peaks, enjoying quiet evenings and calm silent mornings. But by late April the nights were getting cooler and mist on the water in the early mornings warned of coming autumn.

We sailed back down to Whangarei and said our goodbyes and, on my own again, I got on with preparing the boat for the next stage of the journey. She was in as good shape as I could make her but it was a long way and I knew that the miles that lay ahead were likely to be a lot tougher than those I had already covered. I planned to head up to New Caledonia, then on to Vanuatu, before crossing to the north coast of Australia. Beyond Australia the mighty Indian Ocean lay in wait with its reputation for big seas and tough conditions. It had to be crossed if I was to make it to South Africa and on round the fabled Cape of Good Hope.

So one morning in late April I motored out of the estuary as the sun rose over Bream Head and set off on the first stage of the long way home. I turned my course north sailing up the coast I had come to know so well. By sunset, I was passing Cape Brett and it was blowing hard out of the west. I was very sad to be leaving. Once again I felt very much alone. It wouldn't have taken much of an excuse to turn shoreward, head in to the Bay of Islands and maybe stay just another few days. I was sorely tempted but I sailed on into the night and by morning there was nothing more to be seen of New Zealand. I will go back some day.

Cape Brett. My last sight of New Zealand.

The first night of a long passage is always tough for me and over the next few days the weather eased and I got back into the familiar sea-going routine clocking around 150 miles a day and beginning to look forward to the new experiences ahead. On May 3 I sighted New Caledonia and began to thread my way between the many reefs at its south eastern end. I had come 1000 miles in seven days exactly and it had been a good passage. By evening I was anchored in the crowded bay outside the harbour at Noumea. As always, it was a pleasure to get in and safe arrival beers were served. One must keep up traditions. Entry formalities were very straightforward and the people were very helpful. The marina at Port Moselle is pleasant enough and crammed with local boats but it was early in the season and there were few other visitors and, after the friendly family atmosphere of Whangarei, it all seemed a bit sterile. After a couple of days of stocking up on fresh supplies and enjoying the luxury of limitless water and electricity I moved out to an anchorage behind a resort island about three miles to the west, just as the weather broke. It was my 67th birthday and, as usual, I was alone. I lay under grey skies in the lee of the island catching up on sleep and doing lots of odd jobs on the boat as day after day the wind blew and the rain swept over. For six days I saw neither sun nor stars. It was miserable and barely warm enough to sit in the cockpit in the evening. I thought wistfully of home where the days would be getting longer and the promise of the new season lay ahead. There's nothing like living on your boat for three years to take some of the novelty out of it. After six days I had had enough and moved into the main harbour. Next day the wind promptly eased off and the sun came out.

I topped up food and fuel and moved about 30 miles to Prony Bay, a small bay near the southern entrance to the lagoon. Next day I set off for Uvea atoll, a small atoll with a lagoon about a day away, an intermediate stop on the way to Vanuatu. There was a steady enough breeze that held into the evening then freshened briefly under a couple of big clouds before quitting altogether. I motored the remaining six hours to the atoll getting in through the pass at breakfast. Whatever else the French may or may not have done for their colonies, they certainly seem to run the marine side well and even in remote locations you can usually rely on the navigation marks unlike other areas in the Pacific where I have spent many an anxious hour trying to spot buoys and beacons marked on a chart but not actually there.

The lagoon had a beautifully clear white sand bottom but otherwise was featureless with just the very low lying land visible to the east where the identical huts of the standard resort sat in a line on the beach. They were empty. Even though it was in the high twenties and windless it was, officially, winter. The evening was calm and completely silent. The sun went down and the stars came out. With virtually no wind forecast for the coming three days I couldn't see much point in hanging around and next morning I set off across the lagoon and out through the pass which was about seven miles to the west. I was headed for Efate, in Vanuatu, 200 miles to the north. In fact, a breeze did materialise but it came ahead and I wound up beating; something practically unheard of for a cruising boat in the Pacific. The breeze died towards the end of the trip but, even so, I made reasonable time and dropped the hook in the quarantine anchorage in Port Villa 40 hours after leaving.

GALES AND TOOTHACHE

I lay on a buoy in Port Villa for days taking it easy. Port Villa is pretty much like most other small Pacific Island ports with the usual collection of scrappy shops, Chinese stores filled with rubbishy stuff and a local market, although here the streets were tarmac which is quite unusual. There was a tourist trade, mostly from Australia, and the pubs were geared to that along with a couple of Thai massage houses - everything the visiting sailor could want. It was a likeable place and the locals, most of whom seemed to have perfect English, seemed to be naturally kind and pleasant folk. I badly needed to go to the dentist, something I am always a bit wary of in out of the way places, but I need not have worried. The Spanish dentist and his ultra-modern surgery were immaculate and the extraction of the offending tooth and seventy dollars was practically painless.

After six days I headed off again to explore the islands to the north. Perhaps it was too early in the season, perhaps I went to the wrong islands, or maybe I just experienced an unusual spell of wet and windy weather, but to me the islands of Vanuatu seemed to me to be dark, brooding and unwelcoming. They are very heavily forested and the mixture of trees and jungle comes right down to the shore. There are very few beaches. The shore seemed lifeless and silent and it seemed likely that the sights I was seeing were exactly as I would have seen them if I been there centuries ago. The wind blew strongly in between the islands and there were many fierce rain squalls as I made my way north, anchoring at Emae Island, then Epi Island, then over to Gaspard Bay on Malakula, spending the nights lying uneasily in the anchorages.

In Gaspard Bay I managed to get the chain fouled round a coral head. It took a lot of effort to get free and at one stage I thought I was going to have to slip the chain but I got away eventually and sailed over to Smith Cove, on Ambryn Island. The island is said to be haunted and the centre of black magic which is still known to be practiced in the islands. I have an open mind about that sort of thing but whether I believed or not didn't matter. I was quite sure that the locals did and the general atmosphere in the villages certainly seemed strange. I went ashore to visit a village, where the people lived in what seemed to me to be almost squalid conditions without power or running water. Dogs, pigs and skinny chickens roamed at will amongst the huts. It was fairly spooky and after being stared at for a while I went back aboard.

The next day a swell began to roll into the bay and with the wind building and more forecast, I got out and reached back over to Malakula, anchoring in Litslits bay, in between two reefs where other local boats were sheltering. The seaward reefs were very low lying and largely covered at high water so there was little protection from the wind which blew steadily all night. I watched the shore lights anxiously as we sheered about in the gusts. Just after day light, *Beyond* suddenly took off sideways towards one of the reefs. I was up in the cockpit at the time and was able to get the chain up and the boat turned towards the entrance. If I had been asleep I would probably have wound up on the beach. Thank God for a reliable engine.

There was no shelter to be had in the rising wind so I had no choice but to head out to sea in what was now becoming a full gale. The swell breaking on the reefs along the shore was bouncing back to seaward and conditions were fierce as I clawed my way slowly past the headlands. It was pretty awful but I had absolutely no choice. I had my lifejacket on and stayed clipped on even in the cockpit, hand steering much of the time in the bad seas, hanging on as best I could to avoid being thrown across to the leeward side of the cockpit. All day I ran, and reached, in big breaking seas first up the Malakula shore and then across the Bouganville Strait in what were certainly some of the most dangerous conditions the boat and I had been in since leaving home. It got wilder as I got into the area of cross tide on the north side of the coast. By early evening I managed to find bit of a lee to the west of Malo Island and then scooted across another piece of open water into the channel leading to Luganville on Espiritu Santo.

By full dark I was in the lee of the hills and creeping up the shore on the eastern side of the channel. I knew there was some sort of resort further up but I didn't have a large scale chart. I was wet, hungry and tired but very grateful to be out of danger and I made a few passes in as close to the shore as I dared to go, trying to find shallow enough water to get the anchor down. No luck. The deep water seemed to extend right to the beach and I couldn't even make out the water's edge in the pitch dark. As it often was in these waters, the plotter was being unhelpful, telling me I was 50 yards inshore whilst the echo sounder told me I was in 20 metres of water which seemed closer to the truth. Eventually I came to some lights and saw another boat through the rain in the darkness. Casting around slowly with the torch, I spotted a mooring buoy which was almost pulled under by the strong tide ripping past it. I managed to snare it with my chain lasso at the first attempt and sat down in the cockpit with a huge sense of relief. After a while I got into the dinghy and managed to secure a proper line to the buoy almost getting dragged under by the tide as I tried to free the lasso.

When the light of dawn eventually crawled over the hill I saw that I was 50 yards off a jetty at Aore Resort. It seemed good enough for me and I stayed for a week enjoying the security of a mooring and the comforts available ashore. I felt I deserved both. The local people in the resort were delightfully friendly and explained that, although the mooring belonged to them, it has never been tested and so they didn't want to charge me anything to lie on it as long as I didn't mind taking the risk and bought a meal or two from them. It sounded like a good arrangement to me.

Aore was across the strait from the town of Luganvillle and the resort ran a small ferry to take guests and staff back and forwards to town. Port Villa had been a pleasant enough place to be but Luganville had little going for it. It was dirty and dusty and many of the buildings looked as if they had been flung together by a madman with a concrete mixer. I got to know the boatman well and we made several trips back and forward storing up, hauling fuel cans and attending to the many things that needed doing before I was ready to set off on the next leg on the journey to Australia.

I left Aore on a rainy afternoon early in June and motored down the channel. The forecast was for a few days of moderate weather and I hoped for the best but as I cleared the shelter of the land I began to feel the effects of the southerly swell. The black clouds rolled in and the wind gradually gathered strength until by nightfall I was down to the number four headsail with a nasty cross sea running up behind me.

What a great little sail the No 4 is. With the wind on the quarter the boat is being pulled along rather than pushed so there is no tendency to round up so she steers easily and is going fast enough to stay out of trouble. For four days I ran like that in very harsh and wet conditions, knowing I had at least another ten days of this ahead of me and feeling lonely and miserable. Occasionally, the boat would be hit by a few out of sequence seas and would lurch to leeward taking water over the top. With everything battened down it was humid and unpleasant down below but if I tried to open the coach roof skylight she would take one over the top and some water would come down below. After having my bunk soaked for the second time I gave up and sweated it out. I had no appetite, which was just as well, because cooking was an adventure. On a few occasions since leaving Scotland I had wondered what I was doing this for and this was one of them. I often thought back with great pleasure to my happy days in the Pacific and cruising around New Zealand. It did occur to me that if I was a criminal serving time they would not allow me to be kept in these conditions but then criminals don't volunteer to go to prison. One night I was lying in the starboard bunk resting when I became aware of a new noise and thump, just below me every time the boat rolled to starboard. Thumping is always bad news. Sure enough, the batteries had broken the wooden retaining batten that stops them moving laterally and they were on the move.

I managed to re-secure them with lines but only at the expense of drilling a couple of holes in the bulkhead that forms the bunk side, not an easy job in the middle of a very rough night. It was a shame to disfigure the panel but I had to do something. In those first four days we did over 600 miles with just the little headsail up. We were flying.

Eventually the weather eased. Although the sea was still there the wind had lost some of its bite and we made good progress. The speed dropped a bit but it was another couple of days before I set the genoa then eventually the genoa and No 4 together, wing and wing. Nine days after leaving Vanuatu I sighted the light on East Cay reef. I was relieved to make my Australian landfall. Soon I entered the north end of the Great Barrier reef at Bligh Entrance and spent an exhausting couple of days dodging the shipping and the rain squalls, making my way south. Anchoring is forbidden until you have officially cleared inwards so for the solo sailor sleep is at a premium. Eventually, on the afternoon of my twelfth day out, I came to anchor in the lee of Horn Island, where, on payment of a fee $330 and following a quarantine inspection, I was allowed to officially enter Australia. I was astounded by the scale of the fee and so tired I was almost on another planet but I had arrived. Another step along the way and another few thousand miles closer to home.

Advance Australia

Flies, Friends and Crocodiles

BEYOND lay at anchor off the jetty at Horn Island for a week while I slept, ate and generally recovered from the tough trip over from Vanuatu. I was very tired. I think I tended to underestimate the cumulative effects of night after night of tough weather. The poor sleep quality coupled with the continuous background anxiety wore me down. It wasn't the physical effort, because a lot of the time I was simply hanging on trying to eat and rest and waiting for the next thing to go wrong. It was all very different from the easy going routine days and starry nights of the Eastern Pacific.

In Horn Island the tides and currents coming up the east coast of Australia meet those from the Pacific Ocean and the tide rips through the anchorage while the wind blows hard from the southeast every day. Flies swarm everywhere and invade the boat. I only saw one other visiting yacht as most of the cruising boats make their landfalls further down the Barrier Reef and come up the east coast rather than in over the top as I had done.

Horn Island and Thursday Island are considered individual quarantine zones within Australia because of the special ecological significance of the Torres Strait area. Administering to the region has become a growth government industry and uniformed administrators, vets and biologists seem to outnumber the locals, most of whom live on their generous government subsidies and spend their days in the pub playing pool and betting on the dogs and horses. Salt water crocodiles sun themselves on the mud flats at low water and there are prominent notices on the pier warning against going too close to the edge. Everything has to be flown or shipped in and is very expensive and, apart from being the compulsory port of entry for boats coming from the north-east and giving me a chance to see some genuine wild Northern Territory characters in their home environment, Horn had little to offer. After I had recovered some of my reserve of strength I hauled up the anchor and sailed across the Gulf of Carpentaria to Gove.

I had hoped for a quieter passage but it was not to be. The gulf is rough, with the currents from the Indian Ocean to the west creating an unpleasant cross sea, over which the south-easterly blows hard, giving me another rough but fast downwind ride for the 350 miles to Gove.

One day out the pin that locked the monitor clutch into the drum on the wheel sheared its weld and I had to put a bolt in instead. It made clutching in and out a tricky business but it worked. It got so bad one night the galley stove sheared one of its gimbals and did its best to jump across the cabin in the dark. That was fun, because it's heavy, but I managed to secure it with a couple of sail ties. The gas line had not parted so I could still make tea, even if I did have to strap myself in to the galley and hold the kettle in place on the crazily sloping stove. It was all getting a bit wearing to say the least but on the last evening, for no apparent reason, the seas smoothed out and the wind quietened down. Nonetheless, I was glad to get in to the anchorage.

In Gove I met up with the cruising boats which had come up the east coast, missing out Horn Island. It was good to see old friends from New Zealand and some from as far back as Fiji, once again. At one stage there were ten ocean cruisers anchored in the bay and we enjoyed some very social evenings at the Gove Boat Club. A steel boat called *Wanda* arrived with a broken cap shroud and I was able to lend them a length of spectra to perform a temporary repair. We got on well together and spent an enjoyable evening making music on guitar and violin, despite the fact that I cannot read music and so only play by ear. Kevin's wife, Philippa, who was an orchestral violinist, approached her music from entirely the other direction. It's amazing how a couple of rums can lift the standard of a small group. We also got to know an American single hander, Kennedy McLeod, from Alabama, on his way around the world on his double ender *Farstar*. The three boats were to become great friends and we passed many a happy hour in each other's company.

In Gove I first became aware of some of the problems Australia has with its indigenous people. Like many of the Polynesians, Aboriginals have a real problem with alcohol. It seems their metabolism simply can't cope with it. The problem became so serious in the Northern Territories that local laws had been passed preventing anyone buying alcohol in a supermarket or bottle store without a permit, regardless of who they were or from which ethnic group they came. You have to get your permit from the local council offices and the store from which you buy your alcohol enters the permit number into the system so that there is a central record of who is buying what. This means that when someone gets into trouble through alcohol the court can immediately see how much they have been buying, and can impose limits, or withdraw their permit altogether until they learn to behave. It's actually quite a good system but it's a pity that it's needed. There was also a problem in some anchorages with kids stealing dinghies, not because they wanted a boat, but so that they could sniff the petrol in the outboards.

Whilst *Beyond* was on passage to Gove, I had received a series of messages from other boats and from NZ relating to my friends on the historic American Schooner *Nina*. She had encountered severe weather in the
Tasman Sea, on passage from Opua, NZ, to Newcastle NSW, Australia. Nothing had been heard for some days and an extensive air search was underway. Nothing was ever found and it is thought that she was lost with all hands. It was a sad reminder to all of us who heard the news that the sea is still the sea.

Eight boats left Gove on the same morning and our little flotilla headed west, through the notorious "Hole in the Wall" passage on Wigram Island. The passage is a 40 yard wide slot in the solid rock that runs for about a mile. Once you are in there is no way to turn and get out and you have to go through. The tide is fierce and local advice varies as to the best time to enter. One fisherman simply said: "If you find yourself sailing uphill you are stuffed!" Having left Gove ahead of the pack, *Beyond* was the first boat to enter the slot and there was still some foul tide running against me. Unable to turn back, I plugged on with the engine at full revs and it slackened off as I crept through, keeping the others in the picture on VHF. The next boat came through about 30 minutes later and got slack water and by evening we were all anchored in a small bay to the west so there is never a dull moment.

After that things were relatively easy. Over the next few days the fleet split up and visited various anchorages, *Beyond* sailing in company with *Farstar* and 'buddy boating,' as the Americans call it, to Darwin. It was very enjoyable. We didn't visit each other's boats every evening but it made a huge difference to have someone to chat to on the VHF and anchor with in the evening. Kennedy and I were of a similar age and we got on well visiting a few bays together on the way round to Darwin.

I finally arrived in Darwin on July 8 and was directed to a pontoon outside the locks at Cullen Bay to await Fisheries Department inspection. This was necessary because the boat had come from overseas and intended to enter one of the marinas which are protected from the big tides by locks. The authorities are very worried about predatory organisms from overseas being introduced so boats like *Beyond* are put alongside a holding pontoon outside the locks for hull inspection and systems treatment whilst biocide is injected into all the pipes which go through the hull. The seacocks are then closed and the mixture is left to stew for 14 hours. There are large fines if you open the seacocks and the mixture contains dye so that anyone passing can see if you are letting it out. It all sounds a real hassle but, in fact, the whole process was done at no cost and got me two nights free alongside the pontoon. I don't suppose it was too bad for the diver, the standby diver, the safety man, and the clipboard carrier it took to do it either - good old Oz.

The next day I motored round to Francis Bay and locked into Tipperary Waters Marina. It wasn't cheap but a great spot and with showers, laundry shops and a bar. I felt as if I had moved into a five star hotel.

DOWN IN DARWIN

Down and Almost Out

I stayed in Darwin for a month which was longer than I had intended. I had been on the go since leaving New Zealand in April and had already been tired out when I had arrived at Horn Island and since then the coast had not been particularly easy going. It was hot, windy and rough and by the time I reached Darwin I really needed a break. Tipperary Waters Marina provided just that with its laid-back and cruiser friendly atmosphere. There were quite a few boats that I knew from way back and old friendships were renewed and new ones made. Presided over by Keith, the Marina Master, it was for me, miles ahead of the designer glitz and ladies who lunch atmosphere of the hugely expensive Cullen Bay facility just further down the harbour with its massive powerboats, designer people and waterside mansions. On Friday evenings Keith put on a barbeque, to which everyone took food and drink then sat yarning long into the night. Happy times.

You could walk from the marina into town in about 20 minutes which I often did. Just round the corner in the big fishing harbour the fleet were getting ready for the coming season. I enjoyed watching the activity to the background of the roar of portable generators and the scream of cutting discs and clattering steel plate. The fishing must have been profitable because there was an awful lot of money being spent. Darwin was clearly booming.

Australia is a very expensive country and Darwin is one of its most expensive cities. There are huge property developments on reclaimed ground with bars and restaurants and a very upmarket shopping and eating area around the Cullen Bay Marina. The whole place is heavily geared to tourists and priced accordingly and there is a general air of spend, spend, spend about it. If you liked smart coffee bars, hairdressers and restaurants it would have been a great place to be but, in the whole area, there wasn't even a small convenience store or a grocer selling the kind of day to day items one needs to live; certainly not what the average cruising yachties need for whom finding ways to save money is a skill as important as being able to take in a reef. There was, however, one hidden jewel in the form of the chandlery and slipway owned by Darwin Ship Stores. Stepping inside was like being rescued from the world of lunatic consumerism and entering a place where things were as they were supposed to be.

In town the same kind of high spend culture seemed to prevail and the only real trace of the old Northern Territory Darwin I could see were the bunch of sad looking Aborigines hanging around the supermarket, some of whom were pretty drunk and making a nuisance of themselves. It's something of a human tragedy that the original native Australians seem to have been by passed by progress and unable to fit in to the modern Australia. The attitude of some of the modern Australians is less than helpful. At the supermarket one morning I watched an exasperated security man throw an elderly and fairly inebriated Aboriginal out, for the second time in ten minutes. Busy day today, I joked, but had clearly lost his sense of humour.

"I'd shoot the f***in' lot of 'em'," he replied, and he meant it. Just as well he wasn't armed.

After a great week in the marina I moved out to the anchorage in Fannie Bay to anchor amongst the other cruising boats. *Farstar* was there along with *Wanda* and my American mates on *Lardo,* whom I had first met way back in New Zealand almost two years ago. The bay was full of boats massing for the Sail Indonesia Rally. Those of us intending to head west to the Cape were very much in the minority but I had spent years trading to Indonesia in my Merchant Navy days and I had absolutely no wish to go back.

It's so shallow in Darwin that we were anchored well off-shore and the dinghy ride into the sailing club was a long and often wet one so I tended to stay on board. One evening Bill from *Solstice* and I, along with Kennedy from *Farstar,* went ashore to the Darwin Sailing Club and demolished a bottle of Kennedy's very fine malt whisky, which he sneaked in a backpack. Because we were sitting outside the club it seemed only right to buy something so we washed the Scotch down with a few beers from the bar three solo sailors on the toot. What tales were told, what words of wisdom were spoken and sage opinions expressed as the night rolled on.

I had had enough of Darwin and I was anxious to get away before summer with its persistent high pressure set in killing the wind along the northern coasts and making the 2000 mile voyage to Cocos Keeling a slow one. I was feeling a bit better than I had done when I first arrived. One afternoon I said my goodbyes and headed out. I didn't get far. At the entrance I met the swell rolling in and started to hear a new noise. New noises are seldom good news and I eventually traced this one to the bottom bracket for the rod kicker where it joined the mast. Taking a closer look I realised that the rivets holding the bracket to the mast were a bit loose. I was setting off on a passage that would take me right across the Indian Ocean, renowned for its big swell and rough conditions and it didn't take me long to decide that the only sensible course of action was to turn back. That was when the trouble started.

I knew there was a rigger back in Tipperary waters and arranged to dock in to the marina again the following week to get the job done. I decided to move south and spend the weekend at the small anchorage just off the Cullen Bay breakwater, which was a much shorter run ashore in the dinghy, and set off. Darwin harbour is a tricky place. There's a five metre rise and fall of tide and it rips through the shallows and over the bank guarding Fannie Bay. There aren't too many soundings marked on the chart but I had been up and down the bay many times by now and skirted the buoy at the north end if the bank and turned south, but maybe I turned south too soon, or maybe I just wasn't paying enough attention to the track I was making because I came to sudden sliding halt when *Beyond*'s keel touched the sand and we stuck fast. It was very hot, very windy and there was still at least an hour of ebb to go. I could see that the keel had struck a sand ridge and there appeared to be deeper water both ahead and astern. I tried to swing her off with the engine and, when that didn't work, I tied three 20 litre jerry cans of water to the end of the boom and swung it right out to leeward to heel her. But even with my added weight on the end of the boom I had no luck.

A couple of dinghies came by and we took a halyard from the mast head to one of them and tried that but the tide was ripping out and from holding wheel I could tell that the bottom of the rudder was now in the sand as well as the keel. I let the anchor go underfoot to try and hold her because it was clear that we were going to be there a while. *Beyond* was lying quietly, and only heeling a little. Looking over the side I could see that the waterline was about a foot above the water. It was now low water and I felt fairly confident that she would come off without any real damage when the tide began to rise. But this was Darwin.

Sure enough, after a while, the flood began to run in to the bay and a standing wave began to form just off up tide side of the boat. Worried that she might skew round and be driven even further towards an even shallower patch shown on the chart, I let a second anchor go over the stern to hold her. Then the real trouble started. The boat began to roll. I could hardly believe it but she heeled over to one side then rolled back through upright and heeled over on the other. It was scary and there was nothing I could do about it, pinned as I was by the anchors fore and aft. I didn't dare lift the stern anchor in case she swung and started to drag into even shallower water. What had started as a fairly undramatic grounding was starting to take on a more threatening aspect. It was a worry and I put out a securite call on the VHF and made contact with a RIB manned by the volunteer coastguard, hoping that they would be able to take a line and hold *Beyond* head to tide until she floated. They arrived very quickly, came round the stern and motored up the port side then, despite my warning shout, ran straight over my for'd anchor chain which fouled one of their out-boards and stopped them dead. They managed to get clear and moved away to consider their next option. Another yacht was now standing by just up tide of the shallows and the rolling, which had reached alarming proportions, had eased a bit with the making tide.

After another 15 minutes *Beyond* floated and I was able to move the wheel and rudder from port to starboard so everything seemed fine there. She wasn't making any water, but I didn't expect her to, since although she had been pivoting on her keel, there had been no pounding or bouncing. I started the engine again, and with the boat hanging on her for'd anchor, hove in the aft one and stowed it. I wasn't going to attempt to move until I had at least another half hour of flood tide under me and I lay there, quietly, drinking a cup of coffee and talking to the other yacht in the VHF. The coastguard had withdrawn to a tactful distance before anything else happened to them. I thanked them for their help and, a while later with clear water all around me, I hove up the anchor and motored slowly and shamefacedly back to Fannie Bay.

The incident shook me up badly. What was going on? Why had I been so careless? Now what would happen? I was worried about potential damage to the rudder and clearly I needed to get the boat hauled out and surveyed, so I called Keith at the Tipperary and the next day I motored round there giving the bank a very, very wide berth indeed.

Thankfully, Jeff at Cullen Bay slip managed to swop some slipping dates around and at the end of the week we put the boat on the cradle and hauled her out. At first it looked as if all was well, however, a closer examination of the top of the rudder showed a couple of small cracks which would have to be repaired. So out came the rudder and we ground back the glass and Kevlar to get a closer look. A local boat-builder gave us a repair specification which satisfied the surveyor and with Jeff giving up much of his weekend directing operations and doing the technical stuff and me doing the grinding, sanding and general labouring, we had it repaired strengthened and back in in four days. In my discouraged and weary state it was heart-warming to get so much encouragement and cheery advice from someone who clearly wanted to help.

My confidence had taken a bad knock. I was losing vital time and, for a while, I considered forgetting about the Indian Ocean for another year and going north to Malaysia, then perhaps trying to sell the boat in Singapore, but I really didn't want to go north either. After another couple of days settling down I did the rounds of Customs and Immigration then stored up and left heading for Cocos Keeling. *Farstar* and *Wanda* had already gone. It was early August and I was getting left behind by the other boats and in danger of missing the season.

For the first day or so the wind was light and from the south and I sailed along happily in the sun pleased to be back at sea and making progress. I alternated between sailing slowly, motoring in the completely calm patches and stopping and sleeping when there was no wind at night. Boatloads of economic refugees head south towards Australia, hoping to be rescued, and allowed to stay. Australia guards its northern coastline carefully. Every day the Customs Border Control plane would fly over then turn and come around again very slowly, and call me up on the VHF. Last port? Darwin. Next port? Cocos. Number of people on board? One. I was sure they knew it all already and that they would have infra-red imaging which could probably tell them what I had had for breakfast, never mind how many people were on board, but they went through the motions.

Early on the third morning out I tried to start the engine and nothing happened. No power. I cranked it again. The lights dimmed but apart from the futile click from the starter motor relay nothing else happened. I swopped to the engine battery and she turned over and started. Relief. But what had happened to the domestic power? The batteries had been new in New Zealand less than a year ago so surely they hadn't quit? I opened up the locker and soon found out. One of the batteries was bulging slightly and they both had almost dry cells. Not only had I forgotten to check the levels; in my eagerness to fully charge them back in Darwin I had managed to fry them. There was nothing for it but to turn back, which I did, and began to motor slowly east with the wind staying light. If it had come in strong from the east, which was what I had hoped for when I was heading west, I would have been facing a really tough trip back.

Yet again I seemed to have let the boat down and been the architect of my own problems. I was in a very sad and depressed state when the next day the Customs aircraft came over again. Last port? Darwin. Next port Darwin.

I crept back into Fannie Bay just before midnight two days later and the following morning I re-entered Tipperary Waters marina to sort things out. The Customs and Immigration people agreed that I had never left Australian waters so I wasn't charged another $300 and re-inspected.

My friends from Cullen Bay slip came along and we took the batteries ashore for an overnight test.

I was really beginning to wonder about my own abilities. When you start making a series of mistakes such as I had, it's usually a pointer to some other problem. The sailing had been tough since leaving New Zealand and I wondered if the strain was taking its toll. I was underweight, run down and immensely weary. Added to that my enforced stay in Darwin and the unexpected bills, had left me very short of cash to the extent that I was even getting nervous about going to an ATM. I think if someone had come along and offered me a few thousand for the boat I would have taken it gladly and gone home. Thankfully no one did. In the Pacific I had loved the life I was leading, and enjoyed being around the many people I had come to know. But recently I really wondered why I was doing this. Maybe I was losing it, and if that were the case surely I shouldn't be setting off across the Indian Ocean to sail all the way to South Africa? I thought again about diverting to Malaysia and at one stage e-mailed home to say that I might well do that. But the reality was that I would only be putting the problem off for another year, so I determined to carry on. I could after all always divert north after leaving Darwin, provided I didn't have to turn back, yet again.

The final straw came as I was waiting for the batteries to prove themselves able to hold their charge. I was pottering about one afternoon doing odd jobs and greatly looking forward to getting away. I began to feel a bit strange, and a little dizzy and my face started to feel as if it had gone numb. I looked in the mirror and saw that the right side of my face was badly swollen. It was clear that something dramatic was happening in the dental department. I got cleaned up and got a lift up town where I knew there was a dentist, but I arrived just as they were closing for the night. Come back tomorrow and we will see if we can make an appointment, but the dentist is very busy. Good for him I thought, he hasn't got an aching jaw and a face like a football. They gave me the address of another practice, and I set off on foot to look for it, conscious that they too would be closing. I got to the door just as they were getting ready to lock up, and asked for help. I was tired out and in a fair bit of pain. But I realised that my luck had changed when the senior man, heading for the door took one look at me, led me in and sat me down in the chair. His assistant had gone but he got a fresh kit out and took a look. "Abscess in your bottom back tooth, mate. Lucky you got here." He was very interested in the voyage and we chatted for a while. I left with a prescription and an appointment for the next morning to rid myself of the offender. I had always thought that you had to wait for an infection to go down before you could take out a tooth and expected yet another delay, but no, he assured me he would put what he called a "big blocker" in the back. Well that was certainly something to look forward to. Sure enough, next morning after a few skilfully administered injections and some manly wrestling, out it came. Not only that, he so heavily discounted his fee that his secretary thought he had made a mistake. I must have had an air of poverty about me. I heard later that he was known to be the best dentist in Darwin and that it was almost impossible to get on his list. I reflected that if the batteries hadn't failed when they did I would have been half way between Darwin and Cocos when the tooth erupted. Now that would have been a laugh. Yet again, I felt sure that someone was watching over me and I thanked whoever was responsible for these things that I had met guys like Jeff, Keith and the friendly dentist, just when I needed them most. I am a strong believer in fate and somehow quitting and heading north would have seemed like letting them down. Three days later I finally said my goodbyes and got out through the lock. I was sorry to be leaving Tipperary Waters with its friendly atmosphere, but I was glad to be finally on my way. "Take care, mate," shouted Keith. "We enjoyed having you but don't come back." I motored down the channel and out towards the entrance, the wide expanse of Fannie Bay was almost deserted. Everyone else had gone.

18

Darwin Towards Cocos Keeling

Evening Conversations

FOR the first four or five days after leaving Darwin there was very little useable breeze. The standard wind for this part of the world is a fresh southeasterly, such as I had experienced on the way over from Horn Island, and the usual tactic is to leave Darwin on a strong wind warning and get blasted out to the west, then meet up with the steadier Indian Ocean breeze. But I had been late in getting away and the centre of the country was starting to heat up for the summer. The end result was no wind and I knew from the long term forecast that this was likely to be the case before I left, but I had already lost enough time with the various problems I had suffered. I had no choice but to get out there and see what happened. A sobering thought with over 2000 miles of empty ocean between me and my destination.

On the plus side, because it had been calm for so long, there was very little swell, and with a full moon lighting up the sky at night, and extraordinarily clear visibility, it wasn't tough going, just very frustrating and boring. Occasionally, a slight breeze would set in for a few hours and I would get going and creep along for a few miles, before it died and I descended into flapping mode again. But for the most part I motored at about 1500 revs, which gave about 4.5 knots and burnt less than a litre an hour. Several times over the coming three days I would get going again under sail and make a few miles but there was no consistency to the wind at all. It was very hot, the sun rose directly astern and climbed into a cloudless sky beating down all day then setting on a clear horizon ahead before plunging into the sea of glittering gold accompanied by the sound of a sharp hissing as I opened my evening beer, the highlight of the day.

During one twenty four hour period there was not a breath of wind, not even a ripple to be seen. The low swell rolled in, the boat rolled on and the engine droned, never faltering, thank goodness. That would have been the last straw. I took stock of the position and decided that if there was no useable breeze by the following evening I would simply have to stop and lie there waiting for wind and that was not a pleasant prospect. There was none forecast and she would lie beam on to the swell and roll badly. When I got to Cocos, I met a French guy who had spent four days doing this and he didn't enjoy it.

But by late afternoon small patches of ripples began to appear and by evening I had two headsails up on poles and was creeping along in wonderful motorless silence, with only occasional spells of flapping and creaking from the gear. Three knots, four, gradually we got going and by the next morning we were sliding along steadily at just under five knots, hardly record-breaking, but a huge relief, like a slice of bread to a starving man. Every day the border control plane would visit. Usually I would hear it long before I could see it but on some days they would come up low from directly astern and then roar overhead. If I was down below when I heard the first sound I would try and get up into the cockpit before the plane arrived. I didn't want them to think I wasn't paying attention. I got the impression they liked creeping up on yachts and giving them a fright. Then the daily dialogue would start, Last port? Destination? Number of people on board?

One evening the voice on the VHF was that of a lady. "Can you confirm you are the only person on board?"

"Yes," I replied. "Unless you would like to join me," Silence.

"Well you are very kind but I might have a job getting home," she replied. "Exactly. Anyway, drop in next time you are passing."

They rocked the wings and flew off, somehow I felt as if I had made a friend.

After that the wind never left me and stayed well out on the quarter at a steady fifteen to twenty knots, giving some good days runs under twin headsails, including two of 167, and 169 miles respectively.

The sun shone, the monitor steered, the solar panels charged the batteries, the fridge kept the beer cool and all was well. I was eating sleeping and generally living well, with only occasional adjustments to the gear to keep the boat on track. Sometimes the motion would get really confused, as the swell from the Southern Indian Ocean made itself felt and ran across the wind. At times it was far from easy and I had to hang on when cooking and so on but, generally, it was great sailing and I made the most of it. My pal Kennedy on *Farstar* had left Darwin while I had still been coping with dud batteries and dental abscesses and had a lead of about ten days but his boat had suffered in the confused swell and he had broken his gooseneck and diverted to Christmas Island for repairs. We exchanged emails and each morning I listened to other yachts chatting on the SSB about weather and progress. More than one had suffered problems in the rough conditions. There was a quite a mob headed for Cocos with cruising boats coming west from Australia, and coming down south from Indonesia and Malaysia.

So the days went on, twin headsails with one pole on the windward side, occasionally just the one sail at night when it was strong, and the motion was bad. I always preferred to reduce before it got dark rather than have to do it in the middle of the night.

But progress was good and, on the morning of September 2 I sighted Direction Island, entered the channel, picking my way around the coral patches and dropping the hook off the pier around noon. I was glad to be in but, in fairness, after the slow start it had really been a good trip without any serious problems. I had come 2100 miles from Darwin in exactly 16 days.

THE COCOS KEELING ISLANDS

The anchorage at Direction Island is beautiful and completely unspoiled but very windy. Direction Island is linked to Home Island and protected from the sea by a reef on which the swell pounds night and day, providing a background noise of breakers, and sending a fine mist of spray into the air which at times reduced visibility towards the other islands to the South.

The water is absolutely clear and the bottom is white sand with coral patches. It is a bit like being in a floating aquarium, small fish and sharks swim lazily around the boat, and in the evenings dolphins come into the lagoon and roll and leap around. The beach is absolutely white, and hermit crabs scuttle in front of you as you walk.

After a hot windy day late afternoon swimming was a pleasure, but I always stuck close to the beach as there were just too many sharks around the boats in the anchorage. Experienced cruisers would laugh and tell me they were only sand sharks, or reef sharks, or whatever, and that they were harmless but I had no wish to put the theory to the test. I had gone through enough self-inflicted problems in Darwin without voluntarily swimming with sharks, never mind what kind they were. There are a couple of shelters set up ashore, and a rainwater tank, from which you can draw fresh water, but it's far from safe to drink.

There was an interesting gathering of boats in the anchorage and the sailors would gather for beer and barbeque in the evening sitting and yarning away until late by the light of the fire, telling of places they had been and talking over future plans. All of the boats had sailed great distances to get there and, with Swiss, French, Norwegian Danish, American and Scots, we made an interesting mixture of people united in our shared experience and love of cruising. It was a privilege to experience their friendship and talk with them on equal terms.

Here in Cocos I met the Norwegian girls from *Flow*. A doctor and an ex-naval officer, they were an inspiration and nothing seemed to disturb their hugely positive and cheerful outlook. We became friendly and over the coming months the two boats crossed paths in Mauritius and South Africa and again in the Azores. Being in their company always cheered me up and made me feel quite ashamed of my earlier misgivings. There was nothing these two couldn't mend and they did a huge amount of work on their boat. I think if *Flow* had been wrecked somewhere they would just have got hold of some bits, built another boat and sailed on. Vikings indeed. Another Norwegian boat, *Hero*, was sailing with two young children on board and to see the attitude that sailing on a small boat had given these kids was impressive. They seemed completely fearless, would shin up the mast at the drop of a hat and would amuse themselves all day long with very little.

In Gove and Darwin I had seriously doubted the worth of the voyage I was making and had come very close to quitting but here, under the stars in Cocos, I felt that it was a rare privilege to be accepted as part of such rather special band of wanderers and was quite ashamed of the way I had felt a couple of months earlier. I made up a name board for *Beyond* and attached it to one of the trees on which the others have been place over the years, some bearing the names of famous boats whose exploits I had read about 20 or 30 years ago, in the very books that I now carried on board. In a way it was a very humbling experience and gradually some of the excitement and enthusiasm I had felt when I had set off began to return. I stayed in Cocos for six days and then on September 1, *Beyond*, *Farstar* and two other boats hove up, motored out of the lagoon and set sail for the long haul to Rodriguez, 2000 miles to the west.

19

Cocos Islands to Rodriguez

Low Flying on the Indian Ocean Roller Coaster

I had read lots over the years about the passage across the Indian Ocean from Cocos to the west and it was variously described it as rugged, uncomfortable, wet, frightening and exhausting. I soon found out why.

By the end of the first twenty four hours two elements emerged which dominated the coming two weeks; the swell which, with a fetch of thousands of miles rolled up relentlessly from the southeast, and the wind which blew equally relentlessly across it. The result was a wild motion, without any sort of rhythm, making life on board a continuous battle to avoid being thrown across the cabin. The wind rarely dropped below twenty knots and at times blew between twenty five and thirty five for days on end often shifting through twenty degrees and back during the course of a day with the occasional rain squall thrown in to spice things up. Because of the boat's speed in the gusts, the apparent wind sometimes shifted just forward of the beam and, when it did, the water that came over the top was impressive and so was the noise it made.

From the start I kept as little sail up as possible to minimise strain on the boat and make the wind vane's task of steering easier. I had 2000 miles of this ahead and being single-handed, the absolute worst thing that

The swell rolled up from astern

could possibly happen would be for the self-steering to quit. I had long since replaced the steering lines with spectra stripped of its outer cover. It was tremendously strong and, without the cover, I could see at once if any of it was wearing. Apart from it getting a little fluffy where it went through the blocks it never did despite the fact that it was continuously moving and being alternately put under great strain, and then released, over and over again for days and weeks. I doubt if any electric auto pilot could have coped with the conditions for more than a couple of hours. Mine certainly could not even if I could have kept it supplied with battery power. So I left the main lashed securely to the boom and ran and reached, sometimes with the genoa partly rolled in, sometimes with the number four headsail. As the days wore on I rolled the genoa away for good, lashed everything hard in and let her go with the number four.

In the conditions it was important to keep the boat going fast and, with just that very small sail up on the inner forestay, I averaged over 150 miles a day, day after crazy day on the great Indian Ocean Roller Coaster. I would look out of the hatch, and gaze up at the huge crests looming up behind the boat as they marched past and passed harmlessly under the stern. Good old *Beyond,* she handled it beautifully and made my life a lot easier than it might have been. It wasn't very easy to relax and I began to get very tired. On one sunny day I went forward and tried to take some video, but as always, the visual image did little to convey what the conditions were really like. But on the plus side I was making great progress. I was in occasional contact with the other boats and we all seemed to be having the same conditions. Despite the size of the seas and the swell rolling up behind, *Beyond* stayed remarkably dry, taking only the occasional splash into the cockpit; although other boats took quite big amounts of water aboard and I heard later that my Norwegian friends on *Flow* were pushed over sufficiently to have their lee coming under water. But the girls were tough.

By the end of the first week, I had covered 1000 miles. Nothing serious had gone wrong, although I had had a few mishaps; some comical, others less so. The boat would lurch to leeward, then back but with a kind of interrupted rhythm. Sometimes I only got half a lurch, followed by a very fast return then over to windward a little, followed by nose down dash down the face of the swell, as a big one would pick the boat up under the quarter and throw her forwards. This meant that the stuff on the stove would get out of synch with the gimbals and the contents of whatever was cooking would try and keep going in one direction whilst the stove was already halfway back the other way. The kettle flew right off the stove on more than one occasion, denting itself badly, and a pot of stew set off, airborne, across the cabin, and managed to find its way under the chart table where it crashed against the half bulkhead and emptied itself across the deck. Gravy in the bilges. Words were spoken.

I wrote a poem and emailed it home.

The Indian Ocean has a terrible motion, the worst it seems
*   to me,*
Of any I have sailed over before, including the Irish Sea.
There's spray in the air, the waves are all square,
And some come over the top,
Rock roll and sway, it's the same every day.
Wishing to hell it would stop.
Cooking's a chore, never a bore, and seldom easily done
Spill hot tea down your legs, lose control of your eggs,
It's all just part of the fun.
I know that someday, in a land far away,
I will sleep where the soft breezes blow,
But till that day should dawn, I must just soldier on,
Just nine hundred miles more to go.

How I looked forward to that far away and peaceful anchorage.

The days went by, the number four pulled manfully, and I did my best to keep the boat clean dry and in reasonable order as she careered along. There are no leaks whatsoever on *Beyond*. She is as tight as a bottle and no drop of water came down below, other than through my carelessness when I tried to open a hatch to let some air in. I had the blanks on the coach roof vents and most of the time the lower hatch board was in as well. But you can get used to nearly anything and I was able to get into some sort of eating, sleeping, cleaning and maintenance rhythm which, generally, kept me in good shape. There was little else to do. We made fast progress, and on the morning of September 20 we had just 260 miles to go. The instruments told the tale.... Max Wind speed 42 kts. Max boat speed 9.2 knots. No wonder I was feeling the strain. I took photos.

By the twelfth day things had eased a bit. The motion was still wild at times but some of the chaos had gone out of the sea and swell. I needed to slow down to avoid arriving before daybreak so I changed down to the storm jib and we slid along nicely at the required five knots with just 137 miles to go. At daybreak on September 22, I sighted Rodriguez Island. There was still a big sea running and it was blowing hard, as usual, as I headed into Mathurin Bay. I was in touch on VHF with my friends on *Wanda* who were already in and they helped me identify the outer marker for the channel leading in to the harbour.

At 0900 on September 22, *Beyond* was secure alongside the quay in Port Mathurin and 15 minutes later I was sitting in the sun in the cockpit of *Frida*, one of the Norwegian boats already in enjoying a big Norwegian style breakfast complete with a large aquavit. Once again I was amongst friends, again I felt good to be part of this wonderful tribe of wandering sailors, the Bedouin of the watery desert, gathered at yet another peaceful oasis. The day after *Beyond* got in *Flow* arrived. They had had a very wet and rough passage. The boat was soaking down below and one of the girls had been thrown against the hatch, splitting one of the boards. But the girls can cope with anything and before long they had the boat back in shape and had joined in normal life. *Farstar* arrived shortly after from Christmas Island, and before long all but one of the Direction Bay community from Cocos had gathered at the island for some rest.

Rodriguez is a truly charming place, the harbour master could not have been more helpful and would call by most mornings with a cheery greeting and news of the weekly store ship which was due from Mauritius. When the store ship arrived the yachts would have to leave the Bay and go out through the reef then hang around outside so that she could come in through the narrow channel and swing in the bay until she was bows out, then she would tie alongside. Good anchoring spots were jealously guarded and as soon as the yachts saw the ship complete her swing they would dash back up the channel between the reefs and grab a good spot. There was no need to move when the ship left and within an hour or so life had returned to its normal easy pace. Rodriguez, with its village-like atmosphere, was the perfect place to recuperate after the trip from Cocos, and the people could not have been more pleasant. As so often was the case, it seemed that the smaller and more isolated the place the more pleasant the people.

The days passed very pleasantly and after a while the Swiss boat *Andori* arrived, having lost her forestay midway between Cocos and Rodriguez. By then a few of the others had started to move on to Mauritius, a couple of days to the West.

20

Mauritius

Where Every Prospect Pleases and only Man is Vile

I had an easy three day sail over from Rodriguez and docked in the harbour at Port Louis where other boats were already gathered. On the other side of the harbour the might of the Mauritius navy lay in readiness for whatever might come along, although the largest vessel, which I believe had been a gift from another nation, lay idle, allegedly because there was insufficient expertise locally to operate it. There was a small but well established bunch of local guys around the harbour who seemed to have a grip on anything that the yachties might need. They wandered round, constantly watching what was going on and seemed to be in some sort of territorial deal with the marina because the security guards made sure no-one else came around. I hate being reliant on one person for everything but no matter what we would do to get round the arrangement it soon became clear that the best way to get anything done was to accept the situation and get hold of Mr. R. or his mate the laundry man - there seemed be nothing they couldn't arrange.

Anna arrived for a couple of weeks holiday complete with her fins, kitesurfing board and the other accessories required for a holiday in the water. It was a pleasure to have her on board again and see her relax and take a break from work.

The area around the harbour had been completely re developed into a mass of hotels, restaurants and art and designer fashion shops; catering to the tourist trade, which is huge in Mauritius. But step over the road and through the underpass and the crowded pavements, dirty drains and potholed roads made you feel that you could have been in backstreet Mumbai. Some days the smoke and smut of burning sugar fields drifted across the harbour, making a mess of everything and usually there was a fairly comprehensive collection of rubbish floating around in the water, where the little group of cruising yachts in the harbour were a community of their own. *Farstar, Wanda* and *Beyond* were together and *Flow* was close by, along with the stunningly beautiful *Jenni* and the inspirational family team on *Hero*. We all went back a long way and had shared the experience of the tough Indian ocean crossing from Cocos. It made for a crowded and lively quay wall with lots of socialising so we were a little annoyed when the marina management told us we all had to get out because the harbour where we lay against the quay wall had been booked out by the Oyster World Rally which would be arriving in a matter of days. We were invited to move round to the other side of the inner wall and moor up in the creek, where presumably the incoming real sailors on the rally would not be offended by the sight of a group of smaller and very much less ostentatious cruising boats.

I didn't like that idea, so *Beyond* headed north to Grand Baie, a beautiful spot with a very shallow entrance and water so clear that you could easily see the bottom as the boat passed the fairway buoy. With such good visibility it

Grande Baie

was easy to imagine that you were about to run aground as you crept in with the echo sounder showing less than a metre under the keel. We anchored well up into the bay and enjoyed some very relaxing days, wandering around ashore and swimming off the yacht club along with *Flow*. *Farstar* soon arrived to complete the picture.

The cruising community is a bit like a floating village, moving across the oceans according to the seasons. Some stop at one island or in one island group, some at another but, in general, as the cruising year progresses most of the boats will wind up in the same area at more or less the same time. Some cruise in company, some arrange to meet at a future destination and some just keep running across each other. Reputations, good and bad, follow the boats and, like in any small community, tales tend to grow with the telling. Back in New Zealand I had seen one particular American ketch on a few occasions and I was aware of vague rumours about her owner. One afternoon in Mauritius our paths crossed. I was lying at anchor minding my own business when this boat came into the almost empty bay and anchored very close to *Beyond*. I stood up in the bow and watched. The newcomer was so close that had he swung just a little he would have been within a few metres of my bow. Worse, had I wanted to lift my anchor I couldn't have done so because he was sitting right over it. It was strange because there was heaps of room in the bay. I said nothing feeling sure that they would haul up and re-set but they settled down in their cockpit and opened the beers, clearly oblivious to the situation.

I waited for a while then rowed over.

"Good afternoon," I began in what I hoped was my most cordial manner. "I don't want to be awkward but I just wondered why with the whole bay to choose from you have anchored right on top of me."

It was as if I had thrown a grenade into their cockpit.

"You f…….. asshole, this is not close. If you were in California, this is not close, asshole," he delivered in a booming piratical voice. Well well.

"Yes, but we're not in California. This is Mauritius. The whole bay is empty and I still think you are too close," I said.

"I'll tear your f….in' head off, you asshole…….I kill people like you, you…f… asshole." More of the same followed so I rowed back to my own boat. Somehow what had been an almost idyllic spot had lost its appeal and I decided that if they didn't move I would do my best to get my own anchor up and move somewhere else. But sure enough, after a lot of hostile staring in my direction, sanity seemed to return. They hove up and moved away.

I heard later from other boats that the guy had some behavioural problems and often bragged about his exploits in "Nam" and the number of people he had killed.

Two months later, they arrived in Richards Bay in South Africa where loudmouth, apparently unaware that South Africans are some of the hardest guys in the world, or maybe not caring, started a similar line of abuse with a bunch of bikers in a waterside bar. He received a good kicking and wound up in the harbour. Perhaps his hand to hand fighting skills had temporarily deserted him. I occasionally wonder what finally became of him, but not often.

I could happily have stayed a lot longer in Mauritius, but I had to get the boat ready for the last leg across to South Africa. I headed back to Port Louis creeping up the creek in the evening, well clear of the gleaming rally fleet with heir towering masts, blue spreader lights and glittering bright work.

Later that night I put on my best shirt and wandered over to the rally marquee where a cocktail reception of some sort was in full swing. Security had clearly decided they had done enough for the evening and I walked in unchallenged and helped myself to some of the delicious food and wine at the buffet. I felt I was striking a blow for the common man. Luckily, no-one asked me which of the boats I was from.

21

On to South Africa

A Rough Ride

EARLY summer in the Indian Ocean is still a fairly unsettled time as the depressions that form in the Atlantic and sweep past the Cape of Good Hope heading east still have lots of energy. The passage from Mauritius to the South African coast is not one to be taken lightly, with a moderate gale from the northeast often being followed by a stronger one from the southwest as the system moves through.

There were plenty of cruisers' tales of big waves off the coasts of Madagascar and the harsh conditions we might expect crossing the Aghulas current when we got closer to the coast. It's my experience that these tales lose nothing in the telling. Although you have to be aware of the potential dangers, I hoped for the best. Of course, after a few years of mainly downwind ocean crossings we would be sailing upwind for a good bit of the time, but I had already covered over 8000 miles this year since leaving New Zealand and had come through the very testing passage from Cocos to Mauritius, weary for sure, but relatively unscathed so I wasn't particularly perturbed. Everything on board was well tried and tested including the skipper and I felt that there wasn't much we weren't prepared for. I knew that once *Beyond* and I were on the South African coast we would be able to rest before rounding the Cape of Good Hope. Once we had done that we would be back in the good old Atlantic Ocean again with the worst of the homeward journey behind us. Better still, Aurora would be coming to join me in South Africa to sail north to the Caribbean on *Beyond*. It was certainly something to look forward to.

Kennedy on *Farstar* and I had been watching the weather for a week or so and early in November it looked as if there was a reasonable window to get us clear away from the coast and out into open water. On the seventh we sailed down the channel from Port Louis and set off for Africa, planning to make landfall at Durban, about 1700 miles away. There were a few other boats just ahead of us, old friends from further back, and others already nearing the African Coast.

For the first few days things went well, the sky was more or less clear and the sailing was an absolute pleasure. On the fourth day a front came through and the wind backed sharply for a while then shifted back into the southwest. Lots of sail changes for sure and, certainly not the easy downwind sailing I had enjoyed in the Pacific, but I was making progress toward a way point I had set about a 150 fifty miles off the tip of Madagascar. All the books said that it was dangerous to get any closer because of the very difficult conditions that existed when a gale was blowing. It's an interesting thing but in my 40 years of reading about sailing routes and yacht voyages, I have yet to read anything that says you will have a good time.

I skirted the south tip of Madagascar without encountering anything too serious and began the last leg over towards Durban. At this stage I was listening to the daily forecasts from Sam, a retired meteorologist based in Simon's town, who runs a radio net for cruising boats. Yachts making the crossing email their positions every day or so and those who can do so transmit and chat with Sam in SSB. He is a hero to cruising sailors. His forecasts were amazingly accurate and it was a pleasure to hear his quiet, friendly voice as he chatted with the other boats. I could hear all of this, although I could not transmit, and we began to get news of a weather system heading round the Cape which was likely to cause problems for the four boats in our vicinity. One by one the boats further ahead, *Flow* amongst them, reported their safe arrival on the coast and, for a while, it looked as if I might get in and avoid the worst of it but even sailing as fast as I could, I was out of luck. As the low approached I got *Beyond* ready for the blow stowing all the kit below securely and getting everything possible off the decks.

In text book form, the wind strengthened and blew hard from the northeast, and I sat hove to for a while with three reefs in the main and no headsail, watching the barometer drop steadily and listening to the other boats on the radio. Then, late in the evening, the barometer steadied up and the wind died away. With so little wind and a big sea running I started the engine to get her round onto the best heading to meet the new wind which I knew would come in hard from the opposite direction. But I couldn't get any revs out of her.

The throttle cable had parted. Talk about perfect timing! I opened up the engine casing and jammed the fuel pump lever at the right position with a deck shoe and carried on working my way south for a couple of hours until the wind started to build from the southwest and I could sail with the deep reefed mainsail. I knew exactly what was coming. There were four boats within a radius of about 100 miles of each other and it looked as if we were all in for a pasting.

The glass started to rise and the gale came in with a bang and peaked at about 40 knots in the morning. The visibility was almost nil. My world was a mass of grey and as the hours went by the seas built steadily. I sat with the wind about fifty degrees on the bow making about three and a half knots upwind with the monitor steering and the boat rising beautifully to the seas that rolled past. Occasionally, one would break over the deck and I sat under the spray hood watching the scene and drinking tea. Everything was under control. That was until a particularly big wave came over and went straight through the spray hood, demolishing it and tearing the frame right off the coach roof. Being right in the path of the debris, I ended up wearing what was left of it as a hat. Quite a bit of water went down the hatch but at least it was warm. After a while the wind shifted into the SE and began to ease to a steady thirty knots and I was able to bear away a bit and get going towards the coast. It was still uncomfortable. The boat, which had previously been cosy and welcoming below, was now damp and sticky but I was no longer sailing defensively. I was going fast and in the right direction, although without a spray hood it was pretty wet.

Later in the day I went for'd to the bow and set the storm jib and got soaked again in the process. When it's blowing like that, even a small jib makes a huge difference and *Beyond* took off. In my preoccupation with making sure that the boat was ok I hadn't eaten properly in a couple of days and had been living on coffee. I realised I was actually quite weak and starting to shake. Even sitting up in my wet clothes I began to drift into some sort of sleep and I knew I had to eat something fast. To add to the general feeling of being less than 100 per cent, an old problem with my left knee had returned. The joint was swollen and stiff and, all in all, I could have been better. As ever, *Beyond* was taking the strain and looking after me like an old friend. She was the stronger member of the team without a doubt.

Sam warned of yet another weather system on its way so I decided to head for Richards Bay, which by this time was about 18 hours closer than Durban and, late in the afternoon three days later, I arrived. It was blowing hard from the northeast again and there was a big swell. Just north of the entrance the bow section of a wrecked bulk carrier stuck out of the water as if to remind me that this was one of the worst entrances on the coast. I got in and, in sheltered water at long last, I dropped the main and motored round to the marina where my pals from *Wanda,* who were already there waited to take my lines. Sitting with my friends in front of a huge plate of steak and chips and the prospect of an undisturbed night in a steady bunk ahead of me, I felt as if I was almost home.

Only the coast of South Africa and the Cape of Good Hope lay between *Beyond* and the Atlantic Ocean.

It took me quite a while to rest my weary bones and attend to the knee injury, which had me hobbling around for a while, but South Africa is a great country. After visiting the doctor and getting strapped up, I was able to get around not too badly. Richards Bay is a fairly unattractive place but the area around the harbour was developed and something of a magnet for the locals, who came down in droves at the weekend to take in the waterside scene and take advantage of some of the extraordinary deals available on food at the many eating houses. Best of all was eat all you can Saturday breakfast. At which, for a few pounds, you could tuck into mounds of bacon sausage egg, bread toast fruit coffee, etc., etc., and go round as many times as you liked. Families would flock to the harbour from miles around for their weekend treat and we sailors did our best to keep up. It was great.

We watched the weather forecast carefully and when the right window presented itself *Farstar* and *Beyond* headed out and sailed to Durban where we docked in the rather grandly named International Marina. Tucked in a corner of the harbour, the marina was a backwater and seemed to form a catchment for every kind of floating rubbish and general filth. We were warned not to walk out of the gates after dark but the rubbish strewn and crowded streets held little attraction and, in any case, the two Yacht Clubs at the dock were very welcoming. One Friday evening we walked over for happy hour which was crowded with people in their seventies and eighties doing their best to pretend that the old South Africa still existed. At first I thought we had walked into some sort of theme night but, no, this was apparently a standard Friday evening at the club. There was even one gent in some sort of military dress uniform, complete with medals and flowing moustache, who played a selection of suitable melodies on the piano. Strange days indeed.

Over the next two months our two boats made their way round the coast, dodging gales and hiding from bad forecasts first in East London, then Mosel Bay, Port Elizabeth and finally at Simons Town, in False Bay, just east of the Cape of Good Hope.

The South African Coast is very tough going for a single-hander. With one exception, all the passages involve an overnight sail and you have to wait for the right forecast to go. Add to that, the Aghulas current which rips along the coast, the heavy concentration of commercial shipping and the fact that the weather turns almost without warning all adds up to hard going. In addition, many of the marinas are tucked in one corner of what are first and foremost industrial harbours, poorly maintained, dirty and subject to a lot of surge. Often bulk carriers will be working mineral cargoes and dust and grit gets blown across everything. In one port I docked in the dark and walked up the pontoon with torch in my hand to wait for *Farstar*, just a couple of miles behind me. In the space of 20 feet I encountered a very lively rat and some fat but agile cockroaches. I went back to the boat and put some shoes on. But despite the sometimes unattractive surroundings the friendliness of the people was always outstanding.

Simon's Town, however, was the pot of gold at the end of the rainbow and I spent a very pleasant couple of months there getting the boat back into top shape after its hard year in the Indian and Pacific Oceans. I have rarely enjoyed a stopover as much. Apart from being a beautiful place, the False Bay Yacht Club has everything the weary sailor could wish for and the friendly welcome we received from the locals was outstanding. Boats on voyages like mine, "Internationals "as they are known, are given temporary membership status for a nominal fee. There could have been no better place to spend the time and, with the pound being so strong against the SA Rand, I felt for the first time in the entire trip that I had some money in my pocket, or I did until I had my credit card stolen from under my nose in the lobby of the bank. Kennedy made the perfectly innocent mistake of handing his card to the cashier at a filling station to pay for some fuel. Despite never letting the card out of his sight, he spent the next several weeks trying to sort out problems when transactions began to appear on his account from locations all over Africa. We soon learned never to let our cards out of our grasp and

Five solo sailors relax in Simon's Town

L to R: Kennedy McLeod, U.S.A., Dave Isom; Australia; Aurora Canessa, began to visit the bank in twos, with one doing the withdrawal and the other standing behind keeping watch like a constantly vigilant personal protection agent, which, I suppose, was exactly what we were. But upsetting as this was, it was just a tiny flea bite compared to some of the really awful crime that we read about daily and which seemed to be an accepted part of everyday life.

Aurora arrived from Buenos Aires ready for the trip north and we soon got back into our old easygoing relationship and did a bit of exploring in between getting everything ready. Looking at the chart you would think the easiest way to get back to Europe would be to head up to St Helena, then to the Cape Verdes, then over to the Portuguese coast, and if you were in a motor ship that's what you would do. But after St Helena you would be facing headwinds and unfavourable currents. Although some cruising boats take this route, most take the easier, longer route from St Helena then over to the coast of Brazil and then up to the Caribbean, before looping across the Atlantic (again) to the Azores with some calling at Bermuda on the way.

At this time of year you can almost always rely on having moderate wind and current astern from the Cape to Brazil. It's well worth the extra distance and that's what we planned to do.

22

Back in the Atlantic

Two Close for Comfort

WE left Simon's Town and rounded the Cape early in February but only a day and a half out we experienced problems with the engine cooling water and had to put back into Cape Town to sort things out. The Customs and Immigration formalities for clearing outwards from South Africa had been slow and frustrating and, clearing in again, and trying to explain that we had never actually left territorial waters. It was not an easy process but we got there in the end and sorted out the cooling problems by installing a conventional seacock and by passing the sail drive intake altogether. We duly attended the various offices again waited around, presented our documents and eventually got clearance to leave. But South Africa had one final surprise in store. Eight hours after our second departure with a strong south-easterly on the quarter, *Beyond* came off a wave, luffed sharply and the monitor failed to correct. I got into the cockpit as fast as possible and saw that the servo blade had hit something, most probably one of the very large stalks of kelp that floated around, and the shear tube had done what it was supposed to do and parted company with the rest of the gear. It trailed behind on its safety line. I had a spare on board but changing it in the weather conditions we were experiencing was out of the question.

Back again and a 30 mile beat into what had previously been a welcome fresh wind from astern. We crept anonymously into the marina at one in the morning without reporting to Port Control on VHF, slept for five hours and, at first light, I fitted the spare shear tube. We crept out again telling no-one. I like to think that I had finally beaten the system.

For the first three days and nights the strong south easterlies continued with big seas and apparent winds on the quarter in the high twenties. Combined with the following current, it gave us a great start and we managed 167, 183 and 170 miles for the first three days with just a small headsail - good going for sure. After that the weather settled down a bit and we got into a routine of six hours on and six hours off. It might sound a lot to do at one spell but we liked it and in good weather, provided the motion is steady, the time goes quickly and the advantage of six straight hours in our bunks was certainly worth it. But somehow things on board were not just as happy as they should have been and I began to realise that the long voyage ahead might not be as much fun as I might have hoped for. We had certainly spent quite a lot of time cruising together over the last few years but this was the first occasion on which we had sailed together for more than a week and day around the coast with evenings spent in attractive and peaceful anchorages is not the same thing as crossing an ocean. Aurora is a successful solo ocean sailor in her own right and, being of Latin temperament tended to shoot from the hip. With both of us being used to sailing our boats our own way, we occasionally found it irritating to have someone else to consider. It soon began to show.

But the trip rolled on, happy hour generally remained happy enough, the miles slipped by under the keel the sun shone and things could have been a lot worse. The wind eased for a couple of very light days and we motored. At dawn on March 7 we sighted the grim outline of St Helena, its peaks shrouded in rain clouds. By mid-morning we were secured to a buoy in Jamestown Bay, 13 days and 1730 miles out from Cape Town.

Saint Helena

Saint Helena is an island of contrasts. From seaward it has a grim and forbidding appearance, its volcanic peaks shrouded in cloud. There are no beaches, the shore is steep to rocky and heavily fortified and rainsqualls sweep down to the water. No wonder Napoleon felt like giving up hope when he first sighted the place.

In years gone by yachts would anchor off Jamestown, but it's subject to constant swell and several have wound up ashore. In recent years the piracy problem in the Northern Indian Ocean has seen more and more yachts rounding the Cape of Good Hope on their way back to Europe and a field of mooring buoys has now been laid to the south of the port.

Because of the swell and lack of any beach or jetty, there is no possibility of using the dinghy and access to the shore is by a small dilapidated ferry which runs between the moorings and the landing place, a small stone built ledge above which ropes such as we used in the gym at school are rigged. The little ferry runs in with the lifting swell and as she rises you grab a rope and swing ashore, any jerry cans and so on that you have are thrown after you. It's certainly not for the fainthearted. But once ashore, the friendly and welcoming attitude of everyone you come into contact with makes up for the difficulties of getting there. It's a bit like stepping back in time. The manners and speech of the people, most of whom are descended from British soldiers and seamen or from imported labourers, have been uncorrupted by the Americanisms and slang which have become so much a part of the everyday life in Europe. Whilst it seems strange at first, it's actually very refreshing. It was not unusual for locals to approach you in the street and simply ask: "Who are you?"

Inland the countryside is green and pastoral with small herds of contented-looking cattle grazing in the valleys and from the narrow and winding roadside the ocean views were magnificent.

We visited the house where Napoleon had spent his years in exile and where he eventually died, and stood by his grave in a shady and silent glade where he used to walk daily. His remains are no longer on the island, and the grave, surrounded by a simple iron railing, bears no inscription. The English and French Governments could not agree on the wording.

But there are changes afoot. A huge area is being cleared and half a mountain being blasted away to build an airport and a five-star hotel complex and golf course is to be built nearby. In a few years the island will change, as have all remote islands once it simply becomes necessary to pay up and board a plane to get there, rather than to make a long voyage by sea as we had. Coincidentally, of course, the runway will be long enough to take large military transport aircraft and, with the Falklands a key oil and gas reserve, it may be that some of the future tourists have tin hats.

I felt that we were very lucky to experience the island as it is now, and would happily have stayed longer, but the seasons don't wait and after five days on the mooring and numerous acrobatic trips shore we had ferried enough jerry cans of water and diesel out to fill to capacity. Having scoured the shops for what vegetables we could find, we were ready to go and on the afternoon of March 12 we slipped from the buoy and headed off for Fernando Noronha, off the coast of Brazil, as another rainsquall dumped down from the peaks.

HELENA TO FERNANDO NORONHA

We sailed steadily on our way making about 120 miles or so a day, often with both headsails poled and the main stowed. In low apparent wind from stern it's much better to leave the main down, and let the headsails pull the boat along. The barometer is of little use in these latitudes, unless there's something really dramatic about to happen and thankfully in our case it just moved through its diurnal variation each day and the breeze such as it was stayed well out on the quarter as we moved steadily northwest towards our destination just south of the equator. The watches changed and we rolled along, with occasional bouts of flapping, the weather was undemanding and we ate and slept well, despite the heat.

But it was clear to both of us that all was not as it should be between us and we were both glad when, after 13 days or so we sighted Fernando and anchored well offshore. *Beyond* was still rolling and we were conscious of the constant noise of the surf breaking on the rocks. It was an uneasy resting place and hardly an ideal location to try and repair a failing relationship.

FERNANDO NORONHA

When I first looked at the route from S Africa to the Caribbean, I intended to sail direct from St Helena to Grenada but Aurora had called at Fernando some years ago as a stopover on an Ocean race and was keen to go back. Of course, it split an otherwise very long voyage into two more or less equal portions. Fernando Noronha is a Brazilian national marine reserve and, like Helena, has an uncomfortable anchorage and plenty of swell but there the similarity ends. Where St Helena has made a conscious effort to attract and help passing yachts, Fernando seems to have geared itself to attract the very top end of the international air travelling tourist market. Whilst visiting yachts are tolerated, the policy seems to be to discourage them. For the privilege of stopping there the shore authorities charge an entry fee and on top of that a daily fee for each person on board since they are considered to be visiting the reserve. The landing jetty is filthy and crowded with dive boats and there are no facilities in the port area for visitors, other than one public toilet without running water which could be smelt 200 yards away. Welcome indeed.

There is no fresh water available in the port. It all has to be bought at the shop a bus ride away and comes in 20 litre jugs such as you see in water coolers. These are hard to handle off and on the dinghy in the swell so once we had got the jugs to the jetty we decanted them into our own jerry cans then ferried those out. It's a lot of work to fill the tanks and we hired a beach buggy to make life easier. The buggy enabled us to get to the beaches but under recent new regulations all the good beaches have been fenced off and access is via visitor centre gateways for a substantial fee. Once inside you have to hire a guide, who takes you swimming with the dolphins, for a fee, of course. No thanks. We wondered how the locals felt having to pay to visit their own beaches. We did visit a couple of the open beaches but the surf was so heavy and the undertow so strong that even wading to knee depth was dangerous.

I am sure that if you could afford to jet in and stay in one of the many hotels you would have a wonderful holiday. But for cruising voyagers on a budget and used to enjoying the coasts and beaches of the islands they visit, the whole system was less than appealing. To me, the island was simply another step on the way. I remembered the excitement I had felt back in the early days when I looked forward to the prospect of arriving in the Caribbean, then the thrill of getting into the Pacific. But the romance and excitement of the Pacific and the friendliness and fun of New Zealand and Fiji seemed like a distant dream. I was still thousands of miles from home. I felt like a delivery skipper on my own boat and the fun had gone out of it.

We christened the island Fernando Horrible, and left after three frustrating and not particularly enjoyable days, heading North West again, towards Grenada two thousand miles away.

FERNANDO NORONHA TO GRENADA

For the first few days winds were light and the constant swell meant that we spent many an hour flapping along, with barely enough to keep the sails quiet. On one particularly depressing day we managed only 97 miles, the worst day's run ever for *Beyond*. It was hot but, generally, we managed about 120 until on the third day in about one degree south latitude we ran out of wind. We had no choice but to resort to occasional use of the engine. In these circumstances it's always difficult to decide on how long you should keep motoring, and using fuel, before you decide that enough is enough and just stop and wait. But even that has little to recommend it because you could wait a long time, and the boat is never still, constantly rolling and flopping around in the swell. It raises irritation levels and generally makes life miserable, particularly in the heat you experience when its April and you are only just south of the Equator. It would be enough to try the patience of a saint and neither my seemingly increasingly awkward crew nor I were ever likely to achieve that status no matter how hard we tried. We had plenty of food and water but we looked at the diminishing fuel reserves with some concern and, finally, on the evening of the fifth day, with still over 1300 miles to go, we reluctantly decided to head for French Guyana to try and get some diesel. Neither of us knew much about the place, apart from the fact that none of the rumours we had heard were good and access to the river we were headed for was only available at high water.

But, as had so often happened in the past, just when things were looking less than optimistic, a breeze arrived early the next morning and we were off again. We later learnt from two other boats who had called there that things were difficult and that there seemed to be no fuel available. Someone must have been looking out for us.

In order to make the voyage north you have to cross the doldrums of the convergence zone and the limits of the band of calms and squalls move north and south with the seasons. The direct course cuts the zone at an acute angle, prolonging the time you are likely to be in it, and we decided to head in a more northerly direction which would increase the total distance but should shorten the number of windless days.

And so we sailed on the breeze held and, by the time we had reached six degrees north, we were sailing well in apparent wind of up to twenty knots. That was until the inner forestay on which I set the staysail stranded and began to inlay its self from the upper fitting downwards. I got the stay sail down and rolled out some genoa, but the loose portion of the stay was flogging back and forwards hitting the main halyard and the mast above the headboard of the main, in which I had two reefs. I couldn't let it go on doing that and it was clear that I would have to go up the mast which was not a job I relished in the rough conditions. I decided to leave it till the morning and was mentally preparing myself for the task when during the night the loose strands, which amounted to about half the thickness of the stay, jammed themselves between the main halyard and the mast. A perfect solution. It did mean that I couldn't take the reefs out of the main but that seemed a small price to pay to avoid any further damage.

These small day to day problems did little to improve the general atmosphere on board and, in a bid to lighten things up a bit, I made up a number of posters from the pages of a sketch pad showing a smiling face and bearing the words 'No Olivdas sonrir !' Don't forget to smile. At least it got a laugh.

We sailed on but began to suffer from an adverse current which, according to the pilot chart, should not have been there. I have often noticed that the current predictions on these charts are far from accurate, particularly around the outer limits. The data used to compile the charts is in some cases a hundred years or more out of date, and, with changes that are now taking place in the oceans, it's hardly surprising. With 600 miles to go we were well into the northeast trades and had around twenty knots just aft of the beam and were making between 140 and 160 miles a day, even with the reefed main - good going !

Two days out we picked up a favourable current of about one knot and like a tired horse sniffing the stable *Beyond* forged on, and on April 14 she crossed her outward track just south of Grenada and closed the loop. By noon we were swinging on the hook in Prickly Bay, 16 days out from Fernando Noronha.

The champagne cork popped. I was back in Grenada, three years three months and three days after leaving. I had sailed around the world. *Farstar* and *Wanda* were already in and we celebrated together but somehow my heart wasn't in it.

The next day Aurora boarded a plane for Buenos Aires.

23

The Last Lap

Keep Right On to the End of the Road . . .

I had no real urge to hang around in the Caribbean. It had all been new and fun three years ago but now, looking at it after a few years of deep water cruising behind me, it all seemed pretty superficial and in a way a bit grubby. There's a strange atmosphere about some of the islands and I often felt that there was an unpleasant edge just beneath the surface despite the smiles and tourist theatre facade. The boat boys no longer paddle out in old dinghies, they roar out in boats with big outboards and intercept inward-bound yachts when they are still well off-shore. They can be pushy and pretty aggressive at times. I am used to doing things for myself and I don't need anyone to help me onto a buoy or to anchor and I don't like being hustled to pay for things I don't need. Certainly, there's a lot of poverty and many of the young men there have very little in terms of possessions and very little chance of improving their lot. You don't have to look too far back in Caribbean history to see why there could be huge resentment when there are so many relatively affluent Europeans, and even downright wealthy Americans around with fancy boats and all the shiny accessories that seem to be a necessary part of that type of sailing.

There was one robbery related murder on a yacht in Rodney Bay anchorage, St Lucia, just before I got there, and that did little to make me feel at home. Having visited so many countries over the past four years, I find that I become easily irritated by some of the needlessly ponderous Customs and Immigration formalities. With many of the Caribbean Islands belonging to different countries, or being independent, you are often required to clear in and out at almost every island you visit. This becomes farcical if you are only anchoring for the night, as I often did on the way north, so I tried to arrive in the various anchorages in early evening when I knew the offices would be shut and to leave before they opened the next day. Some of the smaller islands are certainly ok and Les Saintes is probably one of the best but some are just not worth the trip ashore and my system seemed to work well, although perhaps no-one really cared anyway.

I worked my way north, as far as St Maarten and rested there for a while. I had been on my own again since Grenada and was quite enjoying my regained independence, having the boat to myself and pottering around getting ready for the solo trip back across the Atlantic. But the spirit was weary. Somehow the dream, or the adventure, or whatever the last three years had been seemed to be over, and I just wanted to get back home and take it easy for a while.

ST. MAARTIN TO HORTA

Like the passage from the Cape to the Caribbean, the voyage from the Caribbean to the Azores is not as straightforward as it looks on the chart. There are two weather systems in play. The Azores High, which moves around within a more or less regular pattern between the islands and the area to the west, and the North Atlantic Westerlies further north above Bermuda.

The rumb line takes you straight through the large area of high pressure and weak and variable winds and, although some yachts load up with fuel, and, if necessary, just push on under engine on the direct route, most try to avoid the calms by heading north until they pick up the Westerlies, then turn east and head for the islands. Some go via Bermuda, to break up the journey, but Bermuda is further west than St Maarten, and I couldn't see the point in heading away from my destination and making the overall trip longer. With all the pressure and wind information now available on GRIBs via satellite phone, you can see exactly where the High is sitting and, if you watch it for a few days before leaving, you can anticipate its movement to the west and then back again. The idea is to look three days ahead, see where the western edge of the system is going to be, and head for that, keeping as far east as you can and easing back off to the west if you start to lose the wind. The end result is a curved course but probably the most efficient way of getting there in terms of sailing. With the boat getting further and further from the trades and into the temperate zone, the barometer becomes important again and it certainly makes for interesting tactical sailing.

After leaving St Maarten, *Beyond* stayed hard on the wind on starboard, managing to keep just east of north and making good progress. Then, after few days of light stuff, the wind backed towards the west letting me head directly towards the western limit of the high pressure area. So I sailed round the high then into the Westerlies, with two days of gale or near gale force wind from out on the quarter. Five days out I got into a very wet and windy pattern with the wind from astern and the log reads, 'very rough sea and big swell, overcast and cold.' I hate wet weather from astern. Because I don't like having the boards in, it all gets a bit damp but we were getting along at a steady 140 miles a day with much reduced sail. I have always sailed the boat cautiously, and I certainly didn't want to risk breaking anything at this stage in the trip, so once a reef was in it tended to stay in. All parts bearing an even strain, as my father used to say.

I wound up more or less on the same latitude as the islands and headed east, making good time and arrived in Horta late in the evening of my twentieth day at sea.

THE AZORES

The islands that make up the Azores belong to Portugal and are a true ocean crossroads for cruising yachts, some of whom are completing an Atlantic circuit, others had travelled from much further afield, as I had. Many of the boats had sailed there from Europe simply for the pleasure of the visit. The authorities are laid-back and friendly, the harbours are clean and the towns are uncrowded, quiet and spotlessly clean.

There is plentiful excellent food and technical assistance of every kind so, not surprisingly, there is always an interesting gathering of cruising yachts in the various ports which makes it a very sociable place to be.

A night in Horta with electricity, water and internet was only eight euros, so many yachts cruise there from Europe year after year.

The islands are volcanic and, although the summer high pressure system can give days of calm around them, close inshore between the islands it can get very windy, indeed, when the cold air drops down from the peaks. My stay there was relaxing and just what I needed after the rather tough trip from St Maarten.

Beyond stayed in Horta for a couple of weeks meeting up with old friends some of whom I had first encountered as long as two years previously, way back up the line in what now seemed like another life entirely. One of the real benefits of being part of the worldwide ocean cruising fraternity is that you make strong and lasting friendships with other sailors and it's always a pleasure to see them again. Some of my most abiding memories are of the wonderful sailing people I had met and I was quietly proud to think that I, too, had ploughed my sometimes lonely furrow across the oceans of the world and become one of them

From Horta I had a very windy day sail round to Terceira, with katabatic squalls off the Island of Pico, whose volcanic peak is so frequently shrouded in cloud. It was baffling sailing. In the space of 100 yards, a gentle breeze suddenly became a squall, the sea turned white and the boat roared along with two reefs and no headsail. Then she would sail out of it and sit entirely without wind in a deep blue millpond whilst 50 yards astern the sea remained wild and steep.

Terceira is another lovely place but windy and it seems to attract far fewer boats, possibly because the harbour is often subject to swell. I was told that as winter approaches all the local boats are moved into the inner recess of the marina and the outer pontoons are disconnected and lifted ashore. Having your harbour in the middle of the Atlantic certainly presents problems and the men who used to launch their longboats from the shore and sail and row out in pursuit of the whales which abound in these waters must have been great seamen.

Gusty winds off Pico

Beyond, fuelled up, watered and well stored, sailed from Terceira on July 2 with the intention of sailing directly to either Spain, or Portugal, about eight days away to the east.

I set off sailing in a generally north-easterly direction on a shy reach. It was grey and overcast but I was getting on fine when, at about six thirty on the second morning, the boat luffed and the headsail started shaking violently. That's usually a wind vane problem but when I got up to the cockpit everything looked normal. The vane had applied correcting helm but nothing was happening. I unlatched the wind vane and put the wheel over to bring her back on course. Nothing. Turning the wheel had no effect on the rudder. My heart sank and I had visions of another major rudder problem such as I had experienced three years before in the Galapagos so I was mighty relieved when I put the emergency tiller on and was able to steer normally. So the rudder was fine. Then it dawned; the connecting rod between the wheel downshaft and the crank on the rudder stock had become disconnected. I dived into the aft cabin and took down the wooden housing on the deckhead which encloses the link arm and, sure enough, the ball joint at its inner end had failed and allowed the link arm to drop clear. I lifted it back up into place and bodged it up with an outsize washer and some Monel wire and, although there was about an eighth of an inch play, the wheel would steer the boat again. If I had been on the middle of the passage I would have made a better temporary fix and carried on cautiously but Punta Delgada on St Miguel lay only 90 miles downwind so I bore away and headed there, creeping into the harbour in the dark at three thirty the next morning.

I had a spare ball joint on board and, with the help of Thomas the local repair guy, by mid-afternoon it was all as good as new. But I wasn't. I was tired so I decided to wait for a couple of days before setting off again. Whilst I was lurking in Punta Delgada, the weather window closed and the wind shifted back into the NE and looked like staying there for a good few days. But I wasn't in a hurry and I had no intention of setting off on what would have been a ten day beat so I made the best of the situation and enjoyed the break. Then *Wanda* arrived. They had also left Terciera with the intention of sailing direct to Europe but had suffered rig problems and, like me, had diverted to Punta Delgada.

I left Punta Delgada on July 10, with the aim of making landfall as far north on the Spanish Coast as I could to give me a good springboard for the Biscay crossing. The first few days were spent sailing quite fast hard on the wind.

It was grey and cold and, for the first time after several years of barefoot and sun soaked sailing, I was having to make sure that I kept warm and dry. I thought fondly of the two years I had spent in the sunny Pacific.

After three days the wind began to ease and the sun came out and by the fifteenth I was doing my best to keep going in near calm conditions.

I finally arrived in Camarinas on the eighteenth, relieved to be back where there were no restrictions on port entry and departure and where I had no need to report with all my documents every time I wanted to check in or leave again. I guess being in Europe has advantages after all.

The wind was due to shift back into the north in a few days and to stay there for a week so I only stayed in Camarinas for 24 hours before heading off to cross the Bay of Biscay. I had a rough and windy but fast trip over the Bay but as I approached Camaret the sun emerged again and things dried out. The heater had been idle for over four years but it started and, for a very encouraging

15 minutes it ran and managed to send a weak but relatively warm stream of air into the cabin. But it stopped and refused to do any more.

Camaret is one of my favourite French ports and it was good to be back. This was around the time of the classic boat festival; the sun shone, and there was a great gathering of traditional craft, much traditional piping, seafood feasting, Breton dancing, accordion playing and wine drinking. I did my best to support the event. After three days in Camaret I took advantage of a fair wind and headed off across the channel to Falmouth, the port I had left the UK from over four years before. I passed the Manacles early the next morning and sailed in bright summer sunshine past Pendennis Point, where my son and my brother stood waving. It had been two years since I had seen them.

I stayed in Falmouth much longer than I had intended, partly because of the arrival of the tail end of Hurricane Bertha and partly just because I liked it there. But I had aimed to be back on the Clyde by the end of August and, after a very pleasant break, I headed down to Penzance, then round Lands' End and over the Bristol Channel to Milford Haven for more reunions with old sailing friends.

Then, across the Irish Sea to Dun Laoghaire, and Howth, dodging gales and getting caught out in a couple of bad days as I made my way further north to Ardglass then Bangor. I was constantly cold and alarmed at the costs of almost everything related to boats and marinas but I was getting closer.

Finally, on the last day of August, I sailed across the Clyde to Largs and docked in the marina I had left four years and 43,000 miles ago.

It had been a long way but I was home.

'Home at last'

Epilogue

IT'S late November and I am back in my little flat on the shores of the Clyde. It's dark and windy and the rain is beating against the window. Writing this account of the voyage and looking at the photographs brings back vivid memories of four of the most fulfilling years of my life. I visited places which, without a boat, I would never have had the chance to see and met some wonderful people whom I would otherwise never have met. Free spirits, living their lives to the full. I am proud to be able to count myself amongst them.

But the geni is out of the bottle. My memory is stranded in the world I have left behind. All of us who have sailed across the oceans owe it to ourselves and our fellow sailors to keep the dream alive.

Someday, I will set off anew and, once again, there will be cocks crowing and dogs barking in the windless dawn, days filled with simple but meaningful tasks and cockpit conversations with friends at sunset.

It will happen.

Stuart MacDonald
November 2014

For Non-Sailors

V.H.F. Very High Frequency radio for short range communications.

G.P.S. Global Positioning System. The satellite-based system use by yachts to fix their position.

A.I.S. Ship identification system. A VHF based system. Yachts carry an AIS to detect the presence of ships and other yachts. Some AIS sets receive only, some transmit as well, so that other vessels will be aware of the yachts position. Connected to an alarm, which sounds if a vessel looks like coming dangerously close.

Sea Me. A system which detects an incoming radar signal and sends out an electronic response which makes the yacht carrying the equipment stand out on the radar of the ship whose radar has been detected.

GRIB File. A type of computer file used to transmit data, such as weather forecasts.

S.S.B. Single side band short wave radio.

Irridium. Satellite based telephone system for voice and data.

Reefing. Reducing sail area when the wind is strong.

Genoa. The large foresail carried in front of the mast.

Staysail. A smaller foresail carried behind the genoa when the wind is strong, or sometimes as well as the genoa when the wind is from astern.

Seas. Waves created by the wind. In calm weather there are no seas.

Swell. Undulation of the water usually caused by larger forces, such as severe weather which may be hundreds of miles away. There is nearly always some swell on the open ocean. When the seas and the swell are running in the same direction, conditions are relatively easy. This is not always the case. Often the wind driven seas will be running across the swell. Sometimes there will be two swell patterns, plus a sea running. This situation is dangerous in strong winds.

Shroud. The part of the rigging that runs from the side of the boat to the mast.

Stay. The part of the rigging that runs from the bow, or the stern, to the mast.

Monitor. Wind vane steering which will steer the boat using only the power of the wind.

Lightning Source UK Ltd.
Milton Keynes UK
UKOW06f1904301115

263853UK00013B/242/P

9 781849 146050